SINGING
AMONG
STRANGERS

Mabel Leigh Hunt

DECORATIONS BY
IRENE GIBIAN

J. B. Lippincott Company

Singing
Among
Strangers

by MABEL LEIGH HUNT

Philadelphia and New York

To

HELEN DEAN FISH

whose radiant qualities of mind and spirit
blessed our long association. She saw the
beginnings of this book and gave to it the
shining beneficence of her encouragement
and enthusiasm.

FOREWORD

THE WINDING OF THE REEL

"As I sang, I wound every song upon a reel." These words from an ancient Baltic folk song might apply to the making of a book.

Early in 1950 I met a newly arrived family of refugees who so excited my admiration and sympathy that a desire flashed up within me to "wind a reel" of stories about their kind. Eventually Lizete, the charming wife and mother, gave me much varied information about her native Latvia, and interpreted for me its mind and spirit, particularly in relation to its traditions. I could scarcely have written this book, as it stands, without her sensitive understanding of my need.

Soon I was meeting other Latvians who were settling in my home city. Among these was the brave and beautiful Anna, who gave me hours of dramatic and inspiring narration. In fact, Lizete and Anna merged in my imagination to become the *mamina* of my story. Young Brona and Agate helped me. It was the latter who remarked, after reading my manuscript: "*Your* family did not have such a bad time." And indeed, had I allowed it to suffer as harshly as did my Latvian friends, readers would probably have considered the story greatly exaggerated.

Singing Among Strangers, therefore, does not record any one person's actual narration. It is a winding of many threads into a single skein—threads from history, from several individual experiences, and from the imagination.

I am pleasantly indebted to Mr. David N. Ross of Indianapolis, formerly Zone Director of the International Committee on Refugees at Salzburg, Austria, for information, literature, and anecdotes relating to the displaced persons' camps in Europe. The Reverend Paul E. Huffman, who has brought hundreds of refugees to America and served them devotedly, appears briefly and inadequately as "Pastor Schoen" in my final chapter.

Planning and writing took a long time. I had to wait until those I wished to interview could speak and understand English, and until they felt assured of the integrity of my purpose. Moreover, I soon discovered that printed descriptions and historical accounts of the Baltics are scant. And as with most English-speaking travelers, my own European itineraries had never included it. Therefore, because my notes were assembled in "bits," and from many scattered literary sources, my bibliography includes only those on which I most relied.

Where is Latvia? Before it was sealed off from the free world by the Soviets, it was one of the Baltic republics, sturdy, progressive, European. Its area was about the same as Holland and Belgium combined. On the west its three-hundred-mile coast line fronted the Baltic Sea. Its continental frontiers lay between Estonia on the north, Lithuania and Poland on the south, and Russia on the east. Its people are Aryans who possess strong native characteristics, yet are somewhat similar to the Scandinavians. They are proud of their political and cultural kinship to the western free world. To a limited extent their country's history is reflected in my story. Regretfully I relinquished the pleasure of retelling their most cherished epics. Neither could I crowd my pages with many tempting folk rhymes.

I wish to emphasize how privileged and responsible I have felt in writing this book. Through those exiles who have become my friends and are now becoming my fellow-Americans, I see them as representatives of a people highly literate and intelligent; of great spiritual dignity as well as of physical beauty. Through their eyes I have glimpsed their native land, and found it lovely. In their personal accounts I have seen human cruelty at its most monstrous, but, on the other hand, human endurance at its most inspiring; the will to survive in dignity; courage, hope, and even the amazing ability to laugh. Through them I enjoy a fresh appreciation of the wonderful gift my country offers to strangers—the gift of America herself. Humbly, I hope those who unwind the reel of this story may experience a renewal of faith in Freedom, and a strengthened determination to help in establishing a free united world.

Mabel Leigh Hunt

Indianapolis, Indiana
November, 1953

1   "IN THE MORNING EARLY"

Lying side by side in their early morning sleep, the two sisters dreamed of flowers. It seemed that they ran through the sunny meadows of Latvia, gathering cornflowers and clovers, wild carnations and daisies. Skylarks fluttered up from under their feet to soar and sing in the blue summits of the sky. The air was sweet with midsummer fragrance.

Marga and Astra opened their eyes. In the first drowsy moment they half-believed that their dreams had come true. But *nē*, it was not a skylark's heavenly singing which they heard. It was only the maid Ruta's voice mingling with the clatter of pans in the kitchen.

"Where are you trotting, my little rooster, in the morning early?" sang Ruta, in the quick *tec, tec, tec* of the Baltic folk song. In a higher key she answered for the rooster. "I am trotting to waken the girls and boys." Ruta's young giggles could be plainly heard.

There was a swish of skirts outside the sisters' bedroom door. "Our mamina comes in a hurry," whispered Astra, and as her mother appeared, she swallowed a hasty yawn.

"Farmer's daughters, do you still sleep?" cried Mamina. "Gailiti our rooster trumpeted the sun into the sky two hours ago. Ruta and I have fed the chickens and the pigs. We have done the milking. Now it is past five o'clock, and time the cows were driven to pasture. And who is to take them?"

"Ruta—" began Astra, lamely.

"Today Ruta will fly like a bee gathering honey, back and forth, to and fro," Mamina retorted. "How fashions have changed in daughters! Why, when I was the child Kristine Baltais, for seven summers I took my father's cows to pasture and herded them the livelong day. Then we had neither fences nor stakes to hold the cows. Those seven summers of duty and delight!" sighed Mamina. "In the peaceful meadows I and my dreams and the long bright day were one. The mittens I knitted; the embroidery I did to enrich my dowry chest! *Jā*, fashions have changed in daughters when this morning they are glued fast to their lazy beds, when they grumble at merely driving the cows to pasture and staking them!"

Suddenly Mamina's mouth began to curve and her eyes to shine. "This is the day! This is the day when we waken with a special joy to midsummer's beauty. Don't you remember? Who shall gather midsummer's flowers and make the wreaths for the merriest festival of the year?"

"St. John's Eve! Ligo Day!" cried Astra, suddenly so wide awake with remembering that she sprang out of bed. She was hastening into her clothes by the time her mother swept away.

"Dear Mamina!" laughed Astra. "How she loves to talk about her childhood in the summer pastures! I wonder, could the herding of the cows have been altogether bliss? Surely not, though this morning our mamina did forget to tell us how she loved to lie lazily among the grasses and gaze at the floating clouds until it seemed as if she, too, were floating. She forgot to tell us how she would sometimes stand on a little hill and, turning slowly, sing to the other hills some beloved Latvian folk song."

"That is what I like to do," answered twelve-year-old Marga, from her pillow. "I sing to the Latvian hills, here in Vidzeme where we live." Softly Marga sang:

> "Blow, little St. John, through
>   the brass trumpet.
> Standing on the hill.
> Let St. John's children
> Gather from everywhere,
> Blow—Ligo, Ligo!"

Marga stretched and yawned, then lay quiet for a moment. "Tonight," she thought to herself, "when everyone is celebrating the St. John's Eve festival, I shall listen closely to the ancient Baltic folk songs. I shall listen, and I shall remember. And tomorrow, when Ligo Day is over, I shall write the songs I like best in my notebook, to keep when I am old, to sing to my grandchildren." Marga smiled, dreamily. To be old—oh, it was a very long time in the future! To be too old to wear the maiden's wreathed crown: too old to dance the Baltic folk dances: too old to watch the night-long fires of St. John's Eve—nē, that was something which could not be imagined! Marga jumped nimbly from her bed.

Presently the sisters, dressed but barefoot, were running through the kitchen. They tossed their braids and pretended not to notice Ruta's teasing look, nor to hear her repeat, "where-are-you-going-little-rooster-in-the-morning-early?"

Spurred by the girls' whacks and proddings, and by the sharp barking of Tonis the dog, the animals filed out from the cow shed. "Hi, Brune! Hi, Princese! Get along, Margrietina! Madam, pick up your proud feet! Hi, Suna!" The girls made their voices laughably hoarse and commanding. Yet, like all farmer folk, they took an affectionate pride in their handsome "Latvian browns."

It was woman's work to care for the cows, the pigs, the chickens, and the vegetable and flower gardens. Kristine Darzins, whom her daughters called *Mamina,* managed the farm, and with the help of her girls and the maid Ruta, did much heavy work. Edvarts, the head of the Darzins family whom his daughters called *Tevs,* was not himself a farmer. He was an engraver and silversmith, and had his own shop in the capital city of Riga, forty-five miles away.

After the first world war, when Latvia become an independent republic, the great estates formerly held by the German land barons were broken up and reapportioned among the people. When Edvarts and Kristine were married, they had applied for a farm. However, for several years they lived on it only during the summer time, spending their winters in Riga. Then Edvarts' parents, Peteris and Zenta Darzins, left their cottage by the sea and moved to the farm to care for the animals. But Grandfather Peteris had died, and Grandmother Zenta, whom the girls called *Vecmamina,* or Granny, decided to share a Riga apartment with her bachelor son, Imants. Uncle Imants worked for a private fishing industry, buying from the fishermen in the little coastal villages and shipping the fish to Riga and other cities. Sometimes he himself went out with the fleets into the Baltic Sea.

So now, except for Edvarts, who came home from Riga only on week-ends and holidays, the Darzins family lived on their farm the year around. And much as they had enjoyed the capital city, with its handsome boulevards, massive buildings, wide busy river and wharves, country life had become more delightful to them.

"Mamina, tell us exactly how you and Tevs met!" For Marga and Astra the oft-heard narrative held a storybook drama in which the right thing happens only by a narrow, but miraculous chance.

"How many more times am I to tell you?" Mamina would cry. But she was never the least reluctant.

"I was Kristine Baltais then." Mamina always began with those words. "I was full of joyous excitement. For I was to take part in my first national singing festival with our choral group from Zemgale. Then, as now, the festival was held every five years, and thousands from the four Latvian provinces were to sing in the great square in Riga which we call The Place of Unity. For many weeks, our group practiced alone, but as the time drew near, we joined with choruses from nearby counties. Your father, Edvarts Darzins, was one of these visiting singers. He sang with the tenors, I with the sopranos." Mamina was likely to pause here, and become dreamy.

"You could tell by Tevs' eyes when he looked at you—" prompted Astra.

"I could tell by his eyes. Well—" admitted Mamina, "he said that I was slender as a linden tree. He said that my silver necklaces were very beautiful."

"He said that your hair was the color of new honey," recited Marga.

"And that your eyes were as blue as cornflowers," Astra chanted.

"Now that is enough," laughed Mamina. "That is how it began with Edvarts Darzins and Kristine Baltais."

But on this summer morning, the girls were thinking of the merry St. John's Eve, as well as their present chore. With Tonis leaping beside them, they staked the cows. Held by long chains to spikes pushed into the earth, the animals could browse, yet they could not stray. Marga gave Brune a farewell pat. "Today, Brune, we shall bring you a present from the little St. John. And one for

Princese, one for Madam, and for Suna and Margrietina," she promised.

Before running back to the house, Astra waved at Mikelis, whom Mamina and the widow Kruze, two farms distant, took turns hiring for their field labor. Mikelis answered Astra's signal with brawny upraised arm as he guided the plow and Gipsy the work horse.

"Now shall we run to the *klets* and beat Cousin Eriks with cat-tails?" Astra's face sparkled with mischief.

Marga laughed. "If Eriks is not already up and about, we will sneak in and beat him until he yells for mercy."

2

HAPPY FAMILY

The small, log-built *klets* was windowless, with a steeply sloping roof. It was used for storage. In summers it made a cool, dark sleeping place. Last night, because Cousin Eriks was a guest, the maid Ruta had given up to him her bed in the Darzins' *klets* and returned to her winter quarters in the farmhouse loft.

Holding their giggles in check, Marga and Astra crept under the foundation of the *klets* to get their hidden sheaves of cat-tails. Then, tiptoeing up the steps of the little building, they slipped through the open door. Outside, the morning danced with light. Inside, it lay silent and shadowy. The stout wooden grain bins along the

8

walls were like squat ghosts. A big cupboard, its doors painted with a design of sun-and-tulips, held the family's best clothing, winter woolens, and festival costumes. There were kegs of homemade wines, pickled mushrooms, cucumbers and sauerkraut. From the rafters Gipsy's Sunday harness and winter sleigh bells hung amid strings of dried vegetables, fruits and herbs. Astra always thought it a pity that the bright birds and leafy sprays painted on Marga's dowry chest were half-hidden in the continual dusk of the *klets*. Grandfather Darzins had made the chest, and in imitation of old-time peasant furniture, he had painted in rather crooked letters the year of its completion, *Anno*, 1937.

On mouse feet the sisters crept toward Eriks' bed. His body lay like a bolster under the covers, for he was a long fellow, being seventeen and tall for his age. Bursting with the laughter they could no longer contain, Marga and Astra began beating Eriks with the cat-tails. He woke with a start, throwing up one arm to shield his head. Then, with a swift, strong motion, he wrenched the covers loose, rolling himself in them as tightly as a caterpillar in its cocoon.

"The St. John's festival is coming, and we beat you with cat-tails!" shrieked Marga, enjoying herself as much as her younger sister.

"Beat all you like!" came, muffled, from Eriks. "Pooh, the cat-tails could be feathers for all I feel them! Sillies, it is not until St. John's Eve that boys and girls beat one another with the tails, and even then it is done only by young city rowdies."

"Then we must be country rowdies, and what if we

are ahead of time?" cried Astra, merrily reckless of both tradition and good manners.

"If you don't get up quickly, Lazybones, we shall eat all the good breakfast. There will not be a crumb left!" Marga's cat-tails swished the air.

Eriks sat up, and with a war cry so fierce it made the girls jump and shiver, he snatched their cat-tails. He threatened to leap out of bed and battle with them. Squealing, half-alarmed but hilarious, the girls fled from the *klets* and along the path toward the house.

But the morning was enchanting, and before going in to help prepare the breakfast, the girls lingered, breathing deeply of the pine-scented, sun-warmed air. Out of sheer joy, Astra ran toward the immense oak which sheltered the house. Eleven years ago her father and Mikelis had leveled off the oak's lofty top, and fastened to it, horizontally, a great cart wheel, to entice a stork to build his nest there.

"Redlegs-who-brings-us-good-luck-and-keeps-away-the-lightning!" Astra now called to the stork which had accepted the invitation. "Do you know, Redlegs, that the sky is blue and not a drop of rain within sight? Do you know that tonight is St. John's Eve, and that every-one in Latvia, young and old, will sing and dance and laugh?"

The strange beady bird-gaze of Redlegs seemed to travel down his long pink bill to rest solemnly on Astra's upturned face. "Child," Redlegs might have answered, "the Darzins' farm has been the nesting place of me and my wife for many summers. But there are other coun-tries. I have flown over them. Little Latvian maid, you

think only of your own land. That is because you have
not wings and cannot fly." And as if to show off, Redlegs, after some awkward teetering on the nest's rim,
raised his great pinions. Away he flew to join his mate
Whitewings, now probing for her breakfast in the marshy
edges of the lake.

Presently, gathered around the Darzins' table, sat
Mamina, the two girls, Cousin Eriks and Ruta. In her
baby chair sat one-year-old Dzintra. Her curls formed a
golden halo around her head. Gleefully she beat an
empty mixing bowl with a wooden spoon.

"Cousin Eriks, did you know that our Dzintra was to
have been a boy named Janis?" asked Astra. "Tevs often
calls her his Janiti."

"Jā, how I prayed for a boy! Yet now Tevs and I have
only daughters." Mamina's mouth drooped sadly. Her
eyes closed as if in unbearable pain. Really, Mamina
should have been an actress! Eriks tipped back his chair.
His mouth opened wide. His laughter rolled out.

The girls laughed, too. But Astra jumped up to shower
Dzintra with kisses. The golden cherub—how happy
everyone had been when she was born! The event was
made completely perfect when Grandmother Baltais suggested that the new baby be named *Dzintra.* It was one
of the loveliest of names, for it meant "amber," and
amber was the "gold of the north," the favorite Baltic
gem.

One summer, on the shores of the fishing village where
her Darzins grandparents lived, Astra had found an amber nugget washed up by the waves. It was large enough
to seem valuable. At first she had treasured it for herself.

But now she was saving it for the day when Dzintra would be old enough to wear an amber-set ring. Astra knew how carefully her father would work on the nugget in his shop. Under the cutting tools and the heat and the polisher, it would glow with a deep, red-gold light. It would send out a faint breath of its long-held balsam fragrance. There was ancient Baltic magic in amber, and luck in the wearing of it. And while the richest deposits of the amber coast did not lie along Latvian shores, Grandmother Baltais, like many others, loved to speak of Latvia as *Dzintarzeme*—"Amberland."

"Oh, how I wish that Grandmother and Grandfather Baltais could have come to celebrate the St. John's festival with us!" mourned Marga at the breakfast table.

"Our grandfather will be host tonight to all his neighbors, because his name is Janis in honor of St. John," Eriks pointed out. "And now that his place is used by the Government as a model farm, Grandfather is very busy. He and Grandmother said that I must take their places here."

"We are always happy to have you, nephew." Mamina had a special fondness for Eriks. Orphaned when young, he had been reared by his grandparents on the farm where Mamina had also grown up.

"You are learning agriculture, Eriks?" asked Mamina. "You like it?"

Eriks' eyes shone. "I shall be a farmer, as are so many in this land," he answered. "The high school I attend runs a student farm. When I graduate, I shall enter the Agricultural Academy at Jelgava. And all the time, I learn from Grandfather Baltais."

"Our grandfather Baltais is important," declared Marga. "Besides being a farmer with rich acres and hired helpers, he is elder of his district."

"And our father, Edvarts Darzins," added Astra, "isn't he one of the most skilled craftsmen in Riga?"

From Mamina came a small scolding sound. "It is true what you say, daughters. But to boast of it makes truth small. Now, let us finish our breakfast. We have much work to do. 'Hard work makes merry holidays,' as the old ones say. And here is Mikelis, who saw the dawn while you were still dreaming. He has already done a half-day's work. He needs his breakfast."

Mikelis, in his farmer's smock and tall boots, grinned good-naturedly from the kitchen door. And closing it against Tonis' eager nose, Mikelis clumped in and took his seat on the bench next to the oven, where he could lean against the bricks and warm the ache in his back.

Astra, over a final spoonful of oats porridge, studied her mother as she filled a mug and plate for Mikelis. "Mamina," began Astra, "I think it is nicest to celebrate Ligo-Janis Day in the country. But no matter how old I become, or how far I shall go from here, I shall remember how it was in Riga. I shall remember because it was so gay and beautiful."

Marga suddenly recalled a snatch from an old folk song. She quoted it gaily, teasing Astra:

"Sing, sing, stranger's daughter,
You are singing among strangers."

"To what strange land do you expect to go, little one?" inquired Mikelis, chuckling into his porridge.

"*Jā!*" giggled Ruta. "To what race of strangers do you expect to sing our songs?"

"I don't, really," admitted Astra. "But sometimes people travel far. Our Latvian president, Dr. Ulmanis, attended a great university in America."

"He fled there when the Russians and Germans suppressed the Latvian revolt for freedom in 1905," explained Eriks. "But now that we have independence and growing prosperity, who would wish to leave our Amberland to 'sing among strangers?' "

"*Nē!* I didn't say I wanted to leave!" cried Astra, indignantly. "I only said—oh, you are all laughing at me! I was only about to describe how beautiful was the midsummer carnival at Riga!"

"We all remember, daughter," her mother assured her. "but now we celebrate in the country. Yesterday we made the St. John's cheese and the honey beer. This morning we must scrub the floors until they are white like snow. While you girls gather the flowers for your wreaths, I will look after Dzintra and do more baking. Eriks and Mikelis will bring boughs from the woods. Who shall say, then, that our house is not worthily decked for St. John's Eve and Ligo Day?"

"Mamina," asked Astra, carrying dishes, "who, exactly, was Ligo?"

"Thousands of years ago," answered Mamina, "before Christ was born and even afterward, our people were pagans who dwelt among the forests and worshipped Nature. One of their goddesses was Ligo. Some call her the goddess of pleasure, and some, the goddess of spring. Others call her the fairy of flowers."

"That is what I like best to call her," interrupted Astra.

"So the people set aside a day to honor Ligo," Mamina went on. "After they became Christianized, Ligo Day became St. John's Day, when earth is greenest and day-light hours are longest, on June the twenty-fourth. But because ours is a very ancient race and our ancient ways live on, we still pay honor to Ligo, the fairy of flowers."

"In honor of Ligo, this year of nineteen hundred and thirty-nine," declared Marga, solemnly, "I shall make my midsummer wreath the prettiest ever."

"According to ancient custom," Mamina pointed out, smiling, "you must gather and weave three-times-nine varieties of blossoms."

"That's twenty-seven kinds!" cried Eriks. "I'm glad I am a boy, and do not need to weave a maiden's wreath."

"*Jā!*" grunted Mikelis. Wiping his mouth of traces of breakfast, he lumbered out of the kitchen.

But golden-haired Dzintra thumped on the bowl. She could have been little St. John himself. *Beat, Janiti, drums of copper, Ligo, Ligo!*

3   ST. JOHN'S CHILDREN

It was hard work helping Ruta to scrub the floors. Push! Stretch! Pull! Swirl!—over and over, while the suds foamed around brushes and bare feet. But when the scrubbing was done, Astra cried out in triumph, "It would not harm our national ballet troupe to dance barefoot on these floors!"

"Now we can gather our flowers, and our minds easy," Marga declared with housewifely satisfaction.

The sisters ran out of doors. Eriks and Mikelis were coming from the forest, so laden with green boughs they looked like trees, walking. It was with a special fulfillment of faith, half-amused, half-serious, that Marga and

16

Astra stopped to watch. First, Eriks and Mikelis fastened branches of the rowan tree to the Darzins' high-arched gate, with its carved symbolic sun motifs and pair of wooden birds perched atop, as on the gates of olden times. Next, they mounted branches on either side of the house doors, and on those of barn and *klets*. Did not the rowan have power to keep evil spirits from house-holders and all their family treasure? Would not the witches, bent on milking the cattle dry on St. John's Eve, be put to flight by the magic twigs?

"Run along, daughters," called Mamina, as she stood in the house doorway with Dzintra in her arms. "You too, Ruta, and on your way, move the cows to new graz-ing places."

Waving a farewell with their empty baskets, and tell-ing Ruta they would catch up with her, the sisters paused for a moment to gaze at the lake which lay below the ter-race in front of their house. It twinkled with a million tiny flashing suns. The girls knew that there were almost three thousand lakes in Latvia, besides many rivers, marshes, peat bogs and drainage trenches. Everywhere was the bright gleam of water.

"The lilies in Sun Lake are open. And look at wily old Redlegs! He stands as still amid the rushes as a stork carved in marble." Marga turned to follow Astra's flying heels.

What a day for gathering flowers to make a mid-summer wreath! What a happy, flowery world in which to be alive, and young! On the borders of the Darzins' fields were cornflowers as blue as the eyes of Baltic maidens. Buttercups and cinnamon flowers, field lilies, primroses and clovers waited for the plucking. The sisters could see other children in the surrounding fields, singing as they filled their baskets. Grandmothers were collecting herbs to dry and hoard for teas, poultices and flavorings. Jā, a sensible old body had great faith in the magic of herbs, gathered at magic midsummer.

A deep, strong voice chanted:

> "I was born singing, and singing I grew,
> Singing I lived my life,
> With songs they escort me
> Into the gates of heaven."

Marga ran forward. "Oldmother, please sing it again!" she begged. "I have heard it before, but not exactly the same." Listening, Marga memorized.

"Those words are as true as can be," Ruta observed, thoughtfully. "All Latvians live their lives, singing."

"Grandmother Baltais has told me that Latvia has more folk songs than any country in the world. We have thousands," boasted Astra.

"Why, of course, sister!" cried Marga. "Everyone knows how through centuries our songs have been our greatest comfort, no matter how we suffered at the hands of cruel invaders. Tevs says that no Latvian needs to keep a notebook of folk songs, because they are written on every heart. Of course I know that," explained Marga, earnestly. "It is only that I dearly love to set down the words of my favorites in my own handwriting."

Astra was thoughtful as she pulled the snowy petals from a daisy blossom. "I think it is nice that you are making your own collection, Marga. I have just now decided to make a notebook of pressed flowers, in honor of Ligo, the fairy of flowers."

"Such a notebook will bring you a Girl Scout badge," answered Marga, smiling.

From a neighboring meadow two boys were beckoning. "Come with us to the forest," called Rudolfs Valters.

"There are bluebells in the woods, and acorns and mosses," shouted Rolands Kruze.

While Astra and Marga entered the forest with the boys, Ruta and Elza, Roland's young-lady sister, waited for them. They sat on a sunlit stump, exchanging neighborhood gossip.

Within the forest it was dark and cool, fragrant with the scent of pine, honeysuckle and deep moist loam.

"In olden times," Marga informed the other children, "the trees were alive the same as people. When a woodcutter entered the forest and made for a tree, it would cry out, 'Oh, Woodcutter, spare my life! Such a poor, crooked one as I will be of little value to you. Yonder tree, which stands so straight and tall, will serve you well.' But when the woodcutter set his axe to the fine, tall tree," continued Marga, her eyes shining in the dusk, "the tree said, 'Listen to reason, Woodcutter! I beg you to take the crooked tree. It will soon rot, anyway, while I shall live to become taller and thicker for you and your axe.'"

Rolands interrupted, his eyes big. "*Jā*, it took a hard heart for a woodcutter of those days to fell a tree, whether straight or crooked."

"And I know why, too," offered Rudolfs. He was a clever boy. His big outstanding ears seemed to catch everything that was said. Now his voice was low with the mystery of the ancient and legendary. "It was because, when the trees were cut, they bled real blood."

"Ooo-oooh!" Shivery giggles came from the girls. Anxious to change the ghostly mood, Astra burst out with an amusing song once taught them by Grandmother Baltais. Marga chimed in:

> "Good morning, forest mother,
> What are your creatures doing?
>
> Rabbit turns the ground up,
> Fox heats the bath,
>
> Woodpecker with the colored coat
> Is tapping tipoo-tapoo."

As if he heard the children mimicking him, a woodpecker drummed loudly above them. Laughing, the girls and boys hastened from the wood. "Tipoo-tapoo!" they called in farewell.

Marga and Astra found their house a bower. Green branches were mounted on the walls. Flowers were strewn on the snowy floors. Bouquets from the garden breathed fragrance—peonies and lilacs, roses and brokenhearts. There was a savory smell of fresh baking.

The sisters and Ruta set to work. They entwined their flowers with leaves from the linden tree, and with *smilgas*, a hair grass gathered from the roadsides. They helped Mamina to plait thick oak wreaths.

By afternoon their father had arrived by bus from

Riga. The girls clung to him, full of affectionate chatter. He tossed up Dzintra, rosy from sleep. He called her his *Janiti*.

Eriks and the girls, carrying grass wreaths, went after the cows. "Brune," said Marga, "here is the present I promised you. It is the largest and finest of our wreaths, because you are our finest and gentlest cow."

The cows had a wonderfully dressed-up look as they plodded toward the sheds, big wreaths caught on their horns or encircling their necks. "See how Madam's wreath has slipped over her eyes," laughed Marga. "She lifts her nose and holds her head proudly, that she may see where she goes, poor beast."

"*Nē*, Madam walks proudly because she wears a crown," answered Astra. "And look at Princese, munching so greedily at Suna's juicy wreath! I do love the crowning of the cows on St. John's Eve!"

"Will Mikelis remember that Gipsy must not be left out tonight?" asked Marga.

"You see Mikelis bringing Gipsy to safety," answered her father, chuckling. "Mikelis knows that on St. John's Eve the devil rides to madness all horses he finds in the fields."

While Mamina, Marga and Ruta did the milking, the men took steam baths in the *pirts*. The greater part of this small, primitive structure extended into the hillside near the lake. It was reinforced with logs. Beyond the low-pitched entrance the dim, cavelike interior smelled of damp earth and soap. When Mamina and the girls took their turns at bathing, they stripped and soaped themselves. Ruta threw lake water on the boulders

piled in one corner, now red-hot from the fire burning
in the pit beneath. Steam rose in clouds. "I dare you
to lie on the highest level among the rafters." But no
one would take Astra's dare. The heat and steam were
intense up there. One could scarcely breathe. The
bathers lay more comfortably on the lower bench, re-
laxing, steaming and sweating. They beat their bodies
with bundles of softened birch twigs. Again they soaped.
They doused one another with clean cold water dipped
from tubs. Dry, and lightly clothed again, they came out
of the *pirts*. The nightingales were warbling among the
lakeside bushes. Mamina's voice had something of the
same musical lilt as she said, "Always we come from
the steam bath with our very souls cleansed."

"Clean enough to wear our national costumes tonight,
Mamina *milumin?*"

Everyone burst out laughing at Astra's angel eyes, and
her honey-tongued way of calling her mother "darling."

"Many will wear their best tonight, Astra *milumin*,"
mocked Mamina. "But the roads are dusty and the fields
damp with dew. Our precious costumes should remain
clean for future wearing."

Inside the house and dressed for the evening, the girls
were sent running to the windows by Tonis' excited barking. "Here come the Kruzes and the Valters," they cried,
whereupon Mamina sang, softly:

> "Dogs bark, guests approach.
> Maiden, run into the room.
> Brush your lovely hair,
> Set your wreath upon your head."

The sisters ran for their wreaths, happy because in Latvia there was a song to fit every occasion. Then all the Darzins stood in their doorway to welcome the neighbors singing at the gate.

The honey beer was passed from hand to hand, followed by the old tuneful phrases of thanks and compliments. Soon it was time to go on. The men's oak wreaths were so thick as to be top-heavy. More big wreaths were strung on their arms. *Kungs* Valters carried his accordion, Eriks his own fiddle. The baskets he and Mikelis bore contained the St. John's cheese, smoked pork, and rye bread. Edvarts Darzins carried baby Dzintra and a rug.

"*Sveiki!* Farewell, holy birds! Guard our dwelling place!" So the Darzins sisters called out to Redlegs and his wife, perched atop the great straw wheel of their nest.

Moving along the road, the procession grew until it arrived at the prosperous farmstead of Janis Bracs. Because St. John's Day was his name day, he was to play host to his neighbors, like every Janis throughout the Baltic lands. He was a tall, jolly Viking. As he appeared with his wife in the doorway of his house, his face was so red with holding back his great laughter and his uproarious singing, that he seemed ready to burst. His eldest son Valdis, whom everyone knew to be sweet on Elza Kruze, stood with his parents.

Marga and Astra, shivering with gleeful expectation, nudged one another. "What fun this is going to be!" whispered Marga.

"It is hard to keep a straight face during all the play-acting," Astra whispered back.

What ridiculous postures the men now struck! What scowling long faces they pulled! With withering scorn they pointed to the fields owned by Janis Bracs. They roared out, in the insulting words of traditional folk song, how his crops were a disgrace to the countryside. "What does he grow in his garden? Weeds! Nothing but weeds! *Shame,* his bee houses are falling into ruin! His barnyard is littered with trash. His cattle are lean and starved. And take a look at his ragged children! Aren't the lice on their heads as big as crawling kittens?"

Oh, the singers were hard on Janis Bracs, and they made up the most shocking falsehoods about him, which everyone enjoyed hugely! As for Janis and his wife, their laughter shook them like jelly.

Now the gestures of scorn changed to sweeping bows, the scowls to smiles, the lies to truth. "Neighbors! Are you blind?" cried *kungs* Darzins. "See, after all, how sleek are Janis Bracs' cattle! How beautifully tilled are his fields, how promising his crops!" The singers poured on the flattery. They called attention to the flowers and greens decking house, gate, and barn. They declared that the *klets* was stored to the rafters with warm winter clothing, with the finest linens, with food and with wine. "But alas, we poor wanderers thirst and hunger! A mug of mead and a bite of St. John's cheese—how welcome they would be!" The crowd joined in singing:

> "Who is a good St. John's mother?
> She who welcomes St. John's children.
> She who is stingy
> Runs back into the house."

So Janis Bracs and his wife roared out a song of invitation. The guests trooped up to crown them with oak wreaths. Staggering under a pyramid of them, Janis led the way to his orchard, where he had set up trestles and benches. From the kitchen *kundze* Bracs and neighbor women carried out great platters of jellied meats; wheat rolls baked with fillings of chopped onion and bacon; pickles, cheese and beer. "Oh, *kundze* Bracs can cook!" sighed everyone with pleasure. Cake was served with the Bracs' famous black currant wine. At last, patting contented stomachs, the merrymakers climbed the nearby hill.

The evening was still bright with the long daylight of the North. The older people joked and gossiped. The young ones played games and pelted one another with flowers and acorns. The maidens' gay skirts whirled, the lads' embroidered belts flew as they danced *The Windmill, The Squire's Polka,* and other familiar folk dances. Songs from every throat poured upward on the golden air. Marga was quick to note the age-old ones. Fiddle, flute and accordion were played. Lighted matches were set to the barrel of tar, high on the pole. The flames shot up in the St. John's fire. From the summits of distant hills burned other beacons. From other merry groups, far away, could be heard echoes of music. "*Ligo, Ligo.* Let St. John's children gather from everywhere."

Another fire was kindled on the ground. Young couples took turns leaping over it. The higher the jump, the taller would grow the grain—barley and rye, oats, flax and wheat. Food from the baskets began to go the rounds. Toward midnight Marga and Eriks, joining a group of young people, took Astra and Rolands and left for the forest which spread itself darkly below the hill. Perhaps someone might behold the miracle of St. John's Eve—the starlike blooming of the fern.

It seemed rather frightening in the woods. Astra and Rolands walked close to Eriks. "And after all," whispered Marga, ruefully, "the only shine I see is from the glow-worm, or the dancing light of the will-of-the-wisp."

But when they had climbed again to the fire-lit hill, a confusion of laughing banter made such a din that Marga and Astra were bewildered. Mamina whispered the explanation. "In the forest Elza Kruze and Valdis Bracs saw the midnight miracle."

Then the girls clapped with the others. For they remembered that it is only lovers, as they plight their troth on St. John's Eve, who see the midnight blooming of the fern. The crowd encircled the happy couple. Representing Valdis, the men sang to his bride-to-be. "Wear your wreath proudly, young girl, but more proudly wear this golden ring of mine."

The women sang for Elza, "This is the last summer I walk dressed in splendor, wearing my wreath."

After midnight, the crowd thinned out, as sleepiness overtook one after another. Of the Darzins family, Mamina, Marga and Eriks remained on the hill. If a person failed to stay up all night on St. John's Eve, he would be a lazy good-for-nothing the entire year.

The sun had scarcely set, in the way of a northern summer night, when it showed red again at rising. With its first rays the festival makers stumbled down the hill and along the roads toward the farms. Marga's eyelids were woefully heavy. Yet, as she staggered homeward, she managed to lift her voice, with others, in a final song:

> "We sang, and sang, and then were quiet,
> There were no songs left to sing.
> We had sung them all,
> We had tired tongues."

4   THE FINE WHITE LOAF

During the feast in the Bracs orchard, Marga had enjoyed a moment's chat with Janis, the friendly host. Because he was a great lover of music and knew a vast number of folk songs, Marga made bold to tell him about her notebook. He could not have guessed how pleased she was with his answer. "You do well, Marga. Our Latvian culture, from earliest pagan times, is revealed in our *Dainas.* Nature as we once worshipped it and today love it; superstitions and customs relating to birth, marriage, and death; the very heart of human experience beats in the rhythm of our folk songs, dances and tales."

And Marga's father had added, "It is a wonderful

thing for Latvia that one of our learned men devoted his life to collecting the *Dainas*. Now we and our children may see them in print, in every school and public library. The volumes are a great national treasure."

Marga hastened to say that she knew about the volumes, but that it was her pleasure to collect the songs she loved best. And as soon as the midsummer festival was past and Eriks had returned to the Baltais' farm, she began to work happily on her notebook. On the flyleaf she inscribed her name. Beneath it she wrote, "These are my songs and the songs of my people. As they sang, in sorrow and in joy, so shall I always try to sing, no matter what happens to me."

Astra thought these words were brave and inspiring. At once she began to gather and mount many native flowers. Mamina even allowed her to walk carefully through the rye, now in beard and taller than Astra. Gleaming amid the stalks were poppies and convolvuluses, mustard and tiny wild pansies.

However, summer on a farm allowed little time for the pursuit of hobbies. In this northern latitude the growing season was brief, but in the strong sunlight the crops of field and garden flourished like tropical plants. So did the weeds. Marga and Astra worked for hours among the vegetables, not only for the home table but for their 4-H club. Each tended her own plot devotedly, so that her troop might outshine all others in later exhibits of giant onions and grandfather turnips.

One morning Mamina would say, "We must gather the cherries before the birds take them." Or, on another day, "If my girls like whortleberry jam, they must run

to the woods with their pails." The work of picking the
small glossy fruit was tedious, but it had also the charm
of a pleasure outing, for there were gay encounters with
other young pickers in the cool, dusky woods. "And I
keep thinking of the jam spread on buckwheat pancakes
next winter," Astra admitted.

The girls also gathered mushrooms. They collected
herbs and roots and seeds for seasonings. In the kitchen
Ruta made the sour black bread for daily eating. But
Mamina made the fine white loaf for Sunday or holiday.
She was unwilling to trust another, even the faithful
Ruta, with the precious wheat flour. Mamina made
and bottled the wines. She pickled the sauerkraut and
the cucumbers. She was forever busy with butter and
cheese-making. There was the daily cooking for the generous table and the eager enjoyment of growing girls.
"Can there be any hungry people in the world, Mamina?"

Even when day was done and neighbors came to chat
on the terrace above Sun Lake, the women and girls
busied themselves with fine needlework. And there was
the constant care of baby Dzintra. She was a joy. She
kept the heart tender and the spirit light.

"The sixteenth will soon be here, Astra," remarked
Marga, one August morning. Didn't Astra know it well,
and that it was the name day (as exciting, but different
from a birthday) of every *Astra*, in whatever province
of Latvia?

"Happy day, grandchild Astra!" cried Vecmamina
Darzins, arriving from Riga as a delightful surprise. "I
have brought you a black silk apron to wear over your

school uniform." Having Vecmamina there was like pleasant old times for the family, and for the neighbors as well, who came bringing bouquets and greetings to Astra, enthroned in her flower-trimmed chair.

When the party was over, Astra and Marga were eager to show Vecmamina all the things she had known when she and Grandfather Darzins had wintered on the farm. With bright-eyed ceremony they escorted her to the orchard. Marga claimed an apple tree as her own. Astra had hers. They had selected one for Dzintra. "Which of the trees do you think will have the largest, finest fruit?" they asked.

How wise and impartial was their granny Darzins! For she answered, "Marga's apples will be very juicy. Astra's apples will have fine, rosy cheeks. Dzintra's apples will drop into her hands like gifts from heaven."

Astra overheard her granny make a splendid suggestion to Mamina. "Astra could go with me for a short visit to Riga, jā?" asked Vecmamina. "She could return safely to the farm with her father next week-end. Would be nice?"

Astra's heart ached with longing for the bus ride which would finally take her and Vecmamina across the pontoon bridge and into the great city. She would walk among the crowds along the Avenue of Liberty. She would see the fruit and flower-sellers in their little booths, and women scrubbing the streets. Again she would visit the twelfth-century "old Riga" that lay like an antique gem within the setting of the modern metropolis, and the tree-shaded parkways and canal which had taken the place of the ancient walls and moat. Tevs would take her to the Brethrens' Cemetery, the splendid war shrine for Latvia's soldier heroes. Perhaps she might ride on a carousel, and attend an American movie, exciting with cowboys and Indians. Or—lovely thought— she might go for a day to the Riga Strand, and run barefoot on the wide beach below the pretty colored villas built on the dunes among the pines. "It might even be," dreamed Astra, "that Uncle Imants would come home to Riga while I am there. He would tell me stories of the sea, and adventures of fishermen."

But Vecmamina returned to Riga without Astra, for Mamina had said, "*Nē*, I cannot spare a single pair of hands. There is much work, and soon the threshers will be coming, and our harvest *talka*. Perhaps next summer you and Marga may visit both grandmothers."

"Work! Nothing but work!" exclaimed Astra, in her disappointment.

"Every worthy Latvian works hard, and rejoices in it," Mamina reminded her, gravely. "In times past, in their serfdom to the barons and the tsarists, our people had nothing but the coarsest black bread. But now, in our freedom, every stroke of work brings us the fine white loaf. Our labor helps not only ourselves, but makes our country strong. That is our aim. Bless Latvia."

Astra was so ashamed of herself that she was glad when Marga called her outside. "We have not seen Redlegs and his wife for two days," said Marga. "I'm sure they must have left for Africa, or whatever winter resort they favor. And almost all the little birds that lived like so many stepchildren in the rim of the great nest have also flown."

"It is a sure sign that summer is about over," answered Astra. Although she knew it was folly, since the storks were not there to hear, she cried out, "Come back next spring, kind birds, and bring us luck for another year." Then she rushed into the house, and slipping her arm around Mamina's waist, she whispered, "Give me something very hard to do, Mamina, for our farm and for Latvia."

There was plenty of hard work! For now came the harvesting of the grain. The Darzins helped the neighbors, each in turn, and the neighbors helped the Darzins. Threshers went the rounds with the great machine. For the sake of tradition, Janis Bracs made a little ceremony on his farm. He had the reapers bind the center oat stalks into one bundle and leave it standing alone in the field. "This sheaf is a home for Jumis, god of the grain," announced the smiling Janis.

"All day long they followed Jumis,
   Hither, thither, through the field.
   Now they've caught him, now they've captured
   Jumis at the center of the field."

Janis roared forth this song with such gusto that the wall of the nearby forest sent back echoes. He did not at first see what was happening behind him. But to his utter astonishment, and to the delight of everyone else, the oats sheaf was seen cutting capers in the field. "It is Jumis himself!" cried the reapers. "Jā, Janis Bracs, your singing has set old god Jumis to dancing!"

"The old god has young feet!" bellowed Janis. With

a sweep of his great arms, he caught the romping sheaf. When he ripped off the binding-stalks, out hopped Rolands Kruze, red-faced, sneezing, giggling.

Jā, that autumn the farmer folk never tired of laughing about the reapers binding Rolands within the sheaf, as a joke on jolly Janis Bracs. Rolands was the envy of all the boys. Even Astra confided to Marga how she wished she might have been the one to play the god Jumis.

So the harvest progressed, farm by farm. At the end of each hard happy day, there was a great feasting. Such bounty as the women and girls cooked and served! Then, in the long summer evenings, there were the *talkas*—the games, the dancing, and the singing of the harvest-time.

> Rye I sow, and barley, too.
> But oats I sow most of all.
> Rye and barley make the loaf fine.
> Oats make sleek the horse's coat.

A song so old, yet—in the round of seasons—new, ever true.

5   A PLEDGE TO DZINTRA

One September morning Mikelis brought from the village a letter from Grandfather Baltais. "Now that the harvest is over," wrote Grandfather, "we shall come for Dzintra's name day. We shall go from Jelgava to Riga. Then, on Saturday next, we shall arrive at your farm. Eriks is coming with us."

On Saturday afternoon, Marga and Astra, full of dancing excitement, waited at the crossroads. At last they sighted the bus, small in the distance, but life-size by the time it pulled to a stop. The three expected guests stepped out, followed by Edvarts on his weekly return from Riga. How wonderful to be swept into Grandfather's strong arms, to be teased as usual by Cousin Eriks, and once inside the house, to know that Grandmother Baltais was within gentle reach, within loving sight and hearing. "Grandmother," confessed Astra, rubbing kitten-like against Grandmother's skirts, "when you and Grandfather are with us in this house, everything has a round and perfect feeling."

So there was the Saturday night steam-bathing in the *pirts*, with eager exchange of talk from the sweating benches. Sunday meant best clothes and attendance at the high-steepled country church. Edvarts rode his bicycle. Eriks and Marga walked. The others rode in the farm wagon. Dinner, shared with the pastor, was a treat of smoked goose, with mushrooms and fresh vegetables.

Chatter, chatter went the tongues of Grandmother and Mamina during the long afternoon of happy family visiting. "A man can't squeeze in a single word," joked Edvarts. So it was scarcely noticed that Grandfather Baltais had little to say.

In the late afternoon, Marga, Astra and Eriks strolled off to bring the cows home. They talked of school, soon to open. Astra proposed a riddle. "What is it—a tall father, a broad mother, a wayward son, a blind daughter?" Marga and Eriks pretended to be puzzled, although the riddle was age-old. Astra reeled off the answer triumphantly. "The tall father is the sky; the broad mother is the earth; the restless son is the weather; the blind daughter is night."

The riddle reminded Marga to tell Eriks of her notebook of folk songs. Then she added, as if she were just that minute making up her mind, "I shall be a music teacher when I grow up."

"Marga!" cried her sister. "How fine it will be to have a music teacher in the family!" She frowned in thought. "What shall I be, I wonder?"

"You need not decide this minute, little one," teased Eriks. "At least neither of you will be a slave to baron or tsarist. But let's talk of something really important—*my* future."

Astra was well acquainted with Eriks' ambition, but it was fun to annoy him a little. "You may become a merchant," she said, making believe, "or a sea captain. You could be a college professor, or a forester, or a soldier."

"Never a soldier!" protested Eriks. "So many wars have been fought on our Latvian soil. So many of our soldiers lie in the Brethren's Cemetery. There is harsh truth in our old proverb: 'Hardly is the father born, than the son is away to the wars.' *Nē*, I want only to be left in peace to work as a farmer."

"You might be Minister of Agriculture some day!" cried Marga, her cheeks flushing in admiration of her tall cousin.

Eriks considered this possibility, seriously. Why not? It was a new age of opportunity in Latvia, now in its nineteenth year of independence and growth. At this very moment, did not a young man's future seem as bright as the light in the high Northern sky?

As the cousins neared the sheds, Astra exclaimed, "Look! Our grandfather walks alone in the orchard.

He is in such deep study I believe it is his brain which paces up and down, instead of his legs."

"I have noticed that Grandfather has been unusually quiet of late," Eriks confided.

"I shall go and cheer him," declared Astra. "I shall show him my pressed flowers. I shall ask his advice on what I shall become when I grow up." Astra ran off for her flower specimens.

When Mamina and Ruta came toward the herd, Eriks took one of the pails. "It is Sunday, Aunt Kristine," he said, "and you do honor to your parents. Let me help Ruta with the milking this evening."

"It is women's work," laughed Mamina. But she gave Eriks a quick pat of thanks as she turned back to the house.

The milk began hissing into the pails. With her head against Brune's flank, Ruta said; "This afternoon, when there was much gay talk, I couldn't help noticing *kungs* Baltais, your grandfather. His mouth was set, as if he feared some old pain, and was bracing himself for another battle with it."

"You and your Sunday fancies, Ruta!" scorned Eriks, lightly. "It is only that Grandfather has many responsibilities in the government of his township in Zemgale. Besides, men his age have grim memories which sometimes intrude on their happy moments. He has told me of living through the terrors of twenty years ago, when our people suffered so dreadfully at the hands of the Germans and Russians. He remembers the bread lines and the 'Communist soup' of those days, the burning and plundering. His own grandfather, forced into heavy labor, died of exhaustion. Grandfather himself almost starved to death. Even as a young boy, you see, he was a victim of foreign invasion."

Ruta's gloom was stubborn. "It has happened to Latvia over and over. It could happen again."

"Over and over, *jā*," agreed Eriks, "because of our geographical position and our coveted Baltic ports. But have you forgotten that we are now a sovereign state belonging to the League of Nations? Ruta, say nothing of your ungrounded fears. Tomorrow is the baby's name day. Let's all be happy."

But that night, at bedtime, Grandfather, whispering a request, drew Marga to the piano. She struck the opening chords of the national hymn, and the family sang together:

> "Bless Latvia, O God.
> Keep her from harm."

"Keep her from harm," Grandfather repeated. It was a prayer.

The girls were ready for bed when their mother called them. "The northern lights are playing. Slip on your robes. Come outside."

The family watched the sky from the terrace above Sun Lake, for its waters gloriously reflected the splendor. The polar beams soared toward the zenith in trembling colored flames, to sink and flicker on the horizon until again they shot upward, and sank and soared again. Said Grandmother, "When I was a child, I was told that the northern lights mean that the souls of our dead heroes still do battle for us in the skies."

When the lights died away and the others trooped into the house, Grandfather laid a hand on Eriks' shoulder. "I would talk with you, grandson, and with you, Edvarts. In spite of our peace treaties with Germany and Russia, in spite of the non-agression pact with the Soviets which they declare to be everlasting, our natural distrust of these two long-time enemies leads us to believe that neither of them can tolerate our freedom and growing prosperity. To them we are so temptingly small. To them our Baltic ports are so alluring. In the past, Russia has called our country her 'window to the west,' or, again, 'a fence which must be knocked down.' Jā, we are Germany's barricade against Russia, and we are Russia's barricade against Germany.

"Now," continued Grandfather, "these two countries have joined in a strange new treaty of friendship. By radio we hear they have invaded our neighbor Poland, from both east and west. Russia has completed three new railway lines in our direction. These enemy movements, stealthy and unexplained, how alarming they seem!" Grandfather sighed, as he added, "I am uneasy."

Eriks' dreams that night were of noiseless but blazing battles in the heavens, with Grandfather leading the host in silent frenzy.

But next morning's sky was so blue and the household so gay that for the time Eriks almost succeeded in forgetting his grandfather's fears. Although it was Monday, Edvarts had stayed at home for his baby's name day. Grandmother had been up with the dawn, for she insisted on making the cake and other refreshments. The girls were glad, for somehow the things that Grand-

mother Baltais made had an incomparable flavor. The
house was soon full of tempting odors. It echoed to
happy flurry. It rang with merry talk and laughter. It
listened with a tender hushed listening as Grandmother
sang to the baby in her arms:

> "All the growing children wondered
> Whence goddaughter came.
>
> Down from heaven she came,
> By little silver chains.
>
> By little silver chains,
> In a silver cradle."

Marga copied this charming song in her notebook,
writing on the margin, "Dear Grandmother Baltais says
she sang this to me when I was little, like Dzintra."

The baby was placed in her small decorated chair.
The Bracs, the Kruzes and the Valters came, bringing
white flowers and small gifts. On the table was the cake,
shaped like the figure eight, and decked with a candle
in each ring. Honey beer and hot chocolate pleased
both grownups and children. There were cold meats,
cranberry sauce, pickled mushrooms, and *buberts*, a
quivering golden custard. Edvarts made a fine little
speech. Marga and Astra played a piano duet. By the
time the last guest had departed, Dzintra was fretful.

Grandmother Baltais took up the baby, patting and
soothing her. But she said to the family, as if she had
only just thought of it, "Not long ago I had such a fright
when I thought I had lost my *sakta*. So I brought it

with me." She left the room, returning with the big brooch in her hand. It was of silver, intricately engraved and set with amber stones.

"Oh, Grandmother!" Astra bounded forward to touch the rich ornament. "You would not have been *you* without your *sakta*."

"Losing it would have been like losing myself," Grandmother declared. "Not only because this was my mother's before me, and a prized personal belonging, but because the *sakta* means to every woman a symbolic sharing in Latvia's folk art and traditions."

It was then that baby Dzintra reached for the shining jewel, too large for her grasp. But Grandmother held the rosy little hand cupped over it, saying, in a kind of farewell way that stirred every heart, "Some day, when I am through with the things of the world, this amber-set *sakta* shall belong to my youngest grandchild, because her name means amber. I pledge it, on her name day."

Grandmother's listeners sighed with a satisfaction half-solemn, half-joyous, for she had made of her pledge a lovely and unexpected little rite. As with all Latvians, they liked their moments to have ceremony and meaning.

Of course the baby did not understand. But there would come a time when Dzintra Darzins would hear how her second name day was made significant by her grandmother's promise. Then she would long for the beautiful *sakta,* as something dear to her lost kin, and as a link to her lost land.

"COLORS"

On a cool October morning, the Darzins' farm wagon, drawn by Gipsy, trundled along the road. It was bound for the rural school ten miles away. Edvarts drove. He was his own master, and on such an important day he had no thought of going to work in Riga. Mamina sat by his side. Marga and Astra occupied the second seat. On his haunches between them sat Tonis the dog.

Astra was excited to the bouncing stage, for this was her first day of school. A Latvian child did not enter the elementary grades before the age of nine, and Astra had only just passed this important milestone. In her new navy blue school uniform, starched white collar

and cuffs, her blond braids neat and shining, she felt
that this was a day she would surely never forget.

Tonis, ears alert, looked as if he might be starting to
school, too. But he was only going along for the ride.
For that reason, however, he was the one creature, except the pigs, which had not been lavishly caressed in
fond farewell by both Marga and Astra. For, like all
rural children who dwelt at a distance, they would live
at the school from Mondays to Saturdays, throughout the
season.

"Mamina," inquired Astra, anxiously, "do you suppose
that the blankets and bed linens we took to school a
month ago are safe and waiting for us?"

"Of course. By this time they are spread on the bed
where you and Marga will sleep together in the girls'
dormitory."

"Do you think my teacher knows that I am coming,
and that this is my first day?" nagged Astra.

"She will be expecting you and the other new pupils."
Mamina's quiet assurance was soothing. And Marga
added, "You know very well, sister, how we registered a
month ago, and your name was entered."

"Astra Darzins." How thrilling had been the sight of
those words, written in the school ledger! And the
names of *kungs* Edvarts and *kundze* Kristine Darzins
topping the page were like sheltering boughs above a
child's head.

"I wonder, now," Astra worried, "if I surely remembered the black silk pinafore that Vecmamina gave me."

Mamina was patient. "That the dignity of the opening
day of school might not be lowered by ordinary matters,

it was last week we brought your extra clothing. We brought also cheese, smoked ham, sugar and flour as our first contribution to the school larder. Surely you remember this."

"Now are you content, little *jaunkundze?*" Tevs turned around with such a look that Astra had nothing to say for some time. But at last, because Marga had been going to school for three years, Astra whispered, "Shall I work in the kitchen?"

"I've told you and told you," Marga answered. "There is but one cook in the school kitchen. She has but one pair of hands. She needs help. Little pupils like you wash the dishes at the end of the day. Older pupils take turns bringing the vegetables from the cellars and preparing them for cooking. These are the vegetables we older ones planted in the school gardens last spring, and weeded and tended throughout the summer. *Jā,* at school every pupil helps."

"I could sweep and dust," Astra offered.

Marga laughed. "Two cleaning women do the sweeping and dusting."

"There is the schoolhouse!" cried Astra, pointing. She stood up excitedly, steadying herself by gripping her father's shoulders. Across the rolling plain the schoolhouse lifted its many-gabled roof. With Gipsy's every step it loomed larger, as did the great wheel of its windmill, its surrounding barns, orchards, gardens and fields.

Other family groups were approaching. "I see Rolands Kruze on his new bicycle," shouted Astra into her father's left ear.

"And there is the headmaster, *kungs* Virzanis, shaking

hands with everyone at the main door," observed Marga. She explained to Astra. "*Kungs* Virzanis lives at the school the year round. See? His house is part of the building. He farms here for his own family and for the school. He attends to everything. This year I shall be in his history class."

"He is all things—a fine man," declared Edvarts.

By the time Astra was out of the wagon and felt her hand clasped kindly within that of the headmaster, she was too greatly overwhelmed by the hallowed import-ance of the day to utter a word.

The children were ushered to their own classrooms. After listening to their teachers' words of welcome, they gathered in the auditorium, where their parents waited. The rural pastor, loved by everyone in his parish, prayed so gently it was like listening to the wind among the pines when one is alone in the forest. The national hymn was sung, all eyes on the flag, crimson-white-crimson. From his high pulpit-like desk the headmaster spoke to the children.

"Today the fine schoolhouses which Latvia has built at great cost, open their doors to many children. Take pride in this one. Listen and study and learn, each of you, that you may grow up to become one more strong link in Latvia's united citizenship. Year by year, we strive to strengthen our land, that she may always stand proudly among free nations. Every child has a responsi-bility toward that splendid purpose."

The children stole glances of pride at their parents. Soon came the time for farewells. To her great surprise, Astra felt her lips trembling. A whole week away from

Mamina, from baby Dzintra, from all the familiar things of home? In her confusion she quavered, "I forgot to kiss Tonis good-bye."

Mamina, with a little laugh, gathered her close. "My linden blossom, going away to school is a part of growing up. Rejoice in it as something precious and important. Work, learn, and be happy, as the headmaster advised." She whispered into Astra's ear, "A mother always leaves a secret little gift to cure the sickness for home. You will find your gift in the cupboard with your slippers."

And Edvarts, after kissing his daughters, called back cheerfully, "I will come for you next Saturday. The week will fly."

If the week did not fly, it did plod steadily along. Marga was a great comfort at homesick moments. So were the special cookies which Astra found near her slippers. The school hummed with activities of work and study. There were many new friends to make. Astra learned the school routine, the shudder and shiver of cold water dousings of mornings, the good hot breakfast, and later a second breakfast. Dinner was served at noon, small refreshments in mid-afternoon, and in the evening a light supper. After dinner in good weather the pupils went with the teachers for walks and games in the woods and fields. When rain and mud were thick they remained in their dormitories or the study halls, and while the classrooms were empty, the cleaning women swept, dusted and aired. For those whose lessons were done, there was play in the late afternoons. Astra learned new games. If given her choice she generally suggested "Colors."

In this game the players chose a head angel, or seraph, and were themselves content to be junior angels. Each was named for a certain color. Now came one lone player, pounding on the heavenly gate—*boom, boom, boom*—and all the junior angels shivered in secret fear and delight.

"Who's there?" demanded the seraph.

"The devil is here, wanting colors," came the dread but expected answer.

"Name the color you want, devil."

"I want black."

"I have no black today, Old One."

"I would as lief have green," declared the devil. Whereupon the little green angel's heart began to thump and his feet to tingle.

"What will you pay for green?" asked the seraph.

"Ten dolders."

"Then," pronounced the seraph, "you must catch my green angel within the time it takes our side to count ten."

So there was the counting, loud, solemn, and fateful, while the little green angel darted in and out among the other angels with the desperate speed of one determined to escape the clutches of the devil. Yet how that Old One flew, his feet winged, his pockets full of money, to catch the green angel!

In this contest between good and evil, which side won? Why, the devil, if he were successful in capturing most of the colors—the lovely green and red and blue, the purple and the gold. But the good side won—*jā—*

if enough glowing little cherubs ran fast enough before
the counting was done!

On Friday nights there was music and marching under
the direction of smiling Zaiga Kimenis, and everyone
the merrier because tomorrow would bring the week-end
at home.

The farm had never seemed more beautiful than on
that first Saturday. Mamina stood in the doorway, Dzintra's curls bright against her shoulder. Ruta, bare-armed,
peeped from the background. There was such a warm
breath of savory simmering and baking as to make a
schoolgirl's mouth water. The last garden flowers glowed
on the table.

Astra was full of chatter about the learning she had
acquired in one week. She described the game of
"Colors."

"Rolands Kruze likes it as much as I do," she declared
with enthusiasm. "Mamina and Tevs, there is a
teacher—"

"Astra has a crush on Zaiga Kimenis," laughed Marga.
"But I am not making fun. Everyone loves *jaunkundze*
Zaiga."

Marga had something to relate. "Tevs, in history class
we have arrived at the sixteenth century, when Tsar Ivan
the Terrible destroyed Livonia, as this our own province
of Vidzeme was then called. The headmaster, *kungs*
Virzanis, appointed certain ones to read aloud. Tevs, the
history made the cold run down my spine and the hot
run into my head. I read aloud the part about the thousands driven into Siberia as prison-slaves, and how the
castles and estates were destroyed until there was little

left in all the land but wild beasts roaming among the weeds and ruins. And I read aloud what one of the bishops of the time wrote to the Pope," said Marga. "He wrote, 'the situation in Livonia is deplorable, the greatness of her sufferings going beyond tears.' There the headmaster stopped me, asking, 'What do you think of that, Marga Darzins?'

"So I answered, 'It is very dreadful, *kungs* Virzanis. But the words of the bishop—I think they are like poetry.'

"Tevs, some of the pupils snorted. So I said, 'Please, *kungs* Virzanis, it is that part—*the greatness of her sufferings going beyond tears*—which sounds like poetry.' And wasn't I glad when he understood!" cried Marga. For he said, 'Class, Marga is right. The bishop's words do sound like poetry, the haunting poetry of Latvia's troubled past.' "

" 'Suffering beyond tears,' " quoted Edvarts, thoughtfully. He slipped his arm around Marga and drew her close.

During these first weeks of school the children heard much grown-up talk. "The pact recently drawn up between Russia and Latvia assures us of better trade relations," said some. Others said, "In the new pact Russia promises to help, should any big power attack us."

"Promises!" snorted Janis Bracs. "What are Russian promises worth?"

And Grandfather Baltais wrote anxiously. "My family, you know there is a new pact. It gives Russia a long-term lease of our naval bases, and permission to establish a garrison of thirty thousand troops. So many Red Army soldiers in our little country? And what about the German residents of Latvia returning to their fatherland in such a hurry? Is it the same as rats which flee a sinking ship? What goes on?"

School was dismissed for Potato Week, when every pair of hands was needed for digging potatoes, one of Latvia's big crops. Presently the first snowflakes were fluttering from the sky. Saturday, November eighteenth, brought Independence Day, the anniversary of the founding of the Latvian Republic in 1918. In their township community house the Darzins joined the crowd. On the stage, beneath the flag and the Latvian coat of arms, amid flowers and lighted candles and bright-berried branches, Tevs and Mamina sang in the mixed choir, "Bless Latvia, keep her from harm."

On the first of December, the Friday night school music was not as enjoyable as usual. "Why are the teachers huddled together in such anxious talk?" asked Marga.

"I know. I heard." Rudolfs' clever listening ears stuck up alertly. "Russia has attacked Finland. I heard *kungs* Virzanis say, 'With Russia and Germany in Poland to our south, and the Russians in Finland to our north, are we to be completely surrounded?'" Rudolfs paused, then added stoutly, "I am not afraid. My father says that Russia knows not the meaning of honor. But the other nations do. They will not allow us to be over-run."

But Marga's thoughts flew to her grandfather Baltais, who was so troubled. "Is the news really true?" she asked her father the next day.

"Riga buzzes with talk about the attack on little Fin-

land," came the answer. On Sunday, the pastor's prayers
filled the church with heart-stirring appeal. Tears were
shed by those who had personal friends among the Finns.

But now the three-day Christmas celebration drew
near. Marga and Astra carried home mittens and muf-
flers they had made in their home-making classes. On
the big farm-sled drawn by Gipsy, they rode into the
forest with their father to select a tree, and set it up in
the house, a silent stranger. But when it was decked
with lighted candles, it seemed to become a friend who
whispered twinkling secrets. It breathed fragrance.
It wore necklaces of colored paper and forest berries.
It held treasures of gilded nuts, apples, and homemade
candies wrapped in fringed papers. Prettily shaped
cookies hung on the twigs. And like any festive Baltic
maiden, the tree wore a crown. It was the star of
Christmas. The holidays were filled with feasting and
neighborly visiting. Rolands Kruze and Rudolfs Valters
had everyone laughing as they trudged from door to
door in animal masks.

Now in winter the half-twilight of the brief days was
brightened by snow and made merry with jingling sleigh
bells. In the pale landscape the birches stood as poised
and delicate as ballerinas in a Christmas pantomime.
The frost man painted his perfect ferns and feathers on
window panes. At school Marga recited a poem beginning, "Spruce and pine have crowns of silver." The poem
sang in her mind like music. She tried to listen to it instead of heeding the heroic but frightful stories coming
out of beleaguered Finland. There, amid deep snows and
bitter cold, the white-clad soldiers were fighting the en-

emy as in primitive battle, hand-to-hand, knife-to-knife.

But . . . "the night is bright with moonlight. Who wants to skate on the lake?"

"I do, Mamina!" . . . "I do, too. Rolands and Elza and Valdis have promised to come and skate with us." . . . "Tevs, you must be the finest skater in all Latvia. Teach us to skate as well." The thrill of skating in the moonlight, cutting through the keen air in long, swift glides, in short, swift whirls—shouting, laughing, singing—and afterward, in the warm house, feeling so sleepy, so-o-o deliciously sleepy!

The days lengthened. The ice softened. It was March of 1940. Across the narrow Baltic Sea, exhausted and diminished Finland signed a treaty with the Soviets. "A high-priced treaty, indeed!" wrote Grandfather Baltais. "But even with all she has lost, praise God that Finland has saved her independence. May our own country—" Grandfather had drawn his pen through this unfinished sentence.

7 JOURNEY AFTER EASTER

Easter fell early in 1940. The pussywillow buds showed no more than gleaming slits of fur. Cousin Eriks arrived for the brief holiday. He brought a chocolate rabbit for Dzintra, and eggs dyed by Grandmother Baltais with beetroot and onion skins. Vecmamina Darzins came from Riga. She taught the girls how to trace Latvian designs on their colored eggs. After church services on Easter morning, the fun began, with exciting egg contests in which Eriks always seemed to win. He ate so many eggs on dares that he pretended to be a hen, sending everyone into gales of laughter with his cackles. "Jā, it is always wonderful when Eriks Baltais comes to the Darzins farm!" exclaimed Ruta.

On Monday Eriks helped Valdis Bracs hang the big Easter swing from a scaffolding on the hills at the Bracs' farm. The neighbors assembled. Gazing upward, they waited to enjoy, on one more Easter, an ancient festal way of greeting the spring.

By turns one couple after another mounted the platform, was given a strong push, and began to swing above the hill. Marga and Rudolfs swung together, Astra and Rolands, Ruta and Eriks, Elza Kruze and her fiancé, Valdis Bracs. In traditional courtesy, each girl presented her partner with a colored egg. Because they had hung the great swing, Eriks and Valdis also received "thank-you" eggs.

Vecmamina, watching, said, "The young people swing high enough for safety. But in my girlhood a couple might go so high they would turn completely over, and yet their feet stay on the platform and their hands on the ropes. I once did it myself, and lived to tell it."

Tall, eighteen-year-old Eriks heard Vecmamina. He stepped forward, his face alive with daring. He called out boldly, "What girl will swing with me, higher than anyone has done today? Who has the courage to swing up and over and down again with Eriks Baltais?"

Scarcely a maid but longed to accept the challenge. Yet—if one's feet slipped at so great a height; if one lost hold in that dangerous somersault! Eriks' spirited glances swept the crowd. He saw the dancing eyes of Elza Kruze. He saw her tense and ready. He cried out, "I need a girl as tall as I am!" And reading the answering flash in Elza's face, he dashed forward and snatched

her hand. Laughing, they leaped to the swing's platform, while Valdis Bracs scowled with jealousy.

Soon the crowd was yelling, "The cows will grow fat!
The crops will grow tall!" For not since Vecmamina's
day, surely, had the Easter swing gone so high, now up
in a great swift climb, now down in a vast sweep, back
to the opposite limit of the arch, down again. Higher it
climbed each time, faster and faster. "They're about to
turn over! Look, they're going—" But the ropes slack-
ened. The platform jolted dangerously as the turnover
failed. Down swept the couple, only to pump more
strongly, to climb higher, faster. "*Jā, jā, jā,* this is a sight
to remember! This is a sight to make the heart stop!
Ligo, the couple is making the complete turn—ah-hhh,
what a perfect somersault, there at the peak of the arc,
there at heaven's summit! Down, now, safely . . .
safely . . ."

"Don't do it any more!" shrieked Astra. *Nē,* she could
not bear to see the somersault repeated, thrilling as it
had been! But the performers had also had enough. Before the swing stopped, Eriks swept Elza off the platform, and bowing, presented her to the stiff-lipped
Valdis. From a basket the girl placed a painted egg in
Eriks' hand. He bowed again.

"Hurrah! Hurrah for Eriks and Elza!" shouted the
crowd. Under cover of the cheers, Astra, glowing with
hero worship, cried, "Cousin Eriks, I will marry you
when I grow up!"

"*Lellite,* my heart is taken," whispered Eriks. His
glance flew to Elza.

So the Easter joy was spent. Vecmamina returned to

Riga. Eriks left, still swaggering a bit, yet faintly troubled with memories of a daring girl riding the sky with him. She was two years older than he—but what difference did that make? She was promised to another—what a great difference that made!

Mikelis came to plow and to plant. The cuckoo and the oriole called from the budding orchard trees, and the Darzins family eagerly awaited the arrival of other guests. "Will the storks return this spring?" . . . "What if something has happened to Redlegs and his mate?" . . . "We shall have no luck if the storks fail us."

But one Sunday morning a great white bird was seen flying high above the earth. "Can it be—oh, let it be Redlegs!" prayed Marga and Astra, gazing intently upward. Now the bird was descending, homeward bound to his summer nest. He alighted on the rim. Folding his wings, he stood solemn and dignified amid the cheers from below. "Oh, Mamina, *must* we go to church?" begged Astra. "Redlegs' wife may arrive, and no one to welcome her. She will think us very impolite."

"We go to church," pronounced Mamina. But after services, among the good-mornings and how-are-you's, the news went around. "The father stork has returned to the Darzins' farm." In the afternoon, a number of the farmer folk came to see Redlegs. They stood smiling and hopeful. While they watched, a pleasant little drama of reunion took place. Out of the southern sky came Whitewings. She alighted, balanced herself, then, weary from her long flight, sank to rest. "See how the mates touch bills, as if in loving greeting," said Astra. And the farmers, a little misty-eyed, but red-cheeked with gladness, cried, "Now the lightning will not strike your roof, Neighbor Darzins! Now all blessings shall be yours!"

Before the first of June the sisters were trying to direct Dzintra's gaze to the storks' nest. "Look, *lellite!* See how the black bills of the two stork babies yap at poor, over-worked Redlegs! All day long he brings them frogs and lizards. Yet never are they satisfied."

Even while the sisters found amusement in the young storks, German bombs were setting western Europe on fire. German armies had invaded Norway, Belgium, and the Netherlands. War was near, indeed. But was not everyone in Latvia feeling easier, because to the east the Soviets were repeating their promises to respect Baltic independence? Marga and Astra were looking forward to attending the national festival in mid-June.

At first Mamina had objected. "There will be such crowds. I cannot look after two young girls, for I shall be one of several thousand singers."

"I will look after them," Edvarts promised. "Our daughters should experience that glory of song. Nothing is more inspiring."

"Shall we see and hear President Ulmanis at the festival?" asked Marga, hugging herself with anticipation.

"He will surely be there. He will talk to us with power and affection, as always," answered her father. "And you girls will enjoy visiting Daugavpils, this year's festival city. It is on our mother-river, the Daugava. Once it was a Viking trading point. Now it is a railway town, into which trains come from all over Latvia, and from Russia and the Ukraine, from Poland and Lithuania. It is also a fortress and the home of our troops."

Right away the festival costumes were tried on to make sure they were in perfect condition. "Oh, Mamina, I know you will be the prettiest singer in all the choir!" cried Marga.

"I go not to show off my costume, but to sing for Latvia."

Mamina's full skirt was ankle-length, woven in soft colored stripes. Her fitted jacket of pale green was sleeveless. The beautiful silver *saktinas* which fastened it had been made by Edvarts. Her white blouse, with long, full sleeves, was hand-embroidered. Her costume, her silver necklaces, her *sakta*, were native to Zemgale, her birthplace.

Marga and Astra, gazing with interest at their own mirrored reflections, tried on their beaded crowns. Their costumes were historically true to Vidzeme, the jackets a strong dark green, the skirts interwoven with beautiful designs. They were careful to put on their plaited silver rings, all the fashion among patriotic young girls, for they symbolized the nation's unity. The rings were copies of one excavated near the site of an ancient stronghold on the Daugava River. Astra and Marga had seen the original in the Historical Museum at Riga.

So the costumes were brushed and pressed and re-hung in the painted cupboard, ready for the wearing on the sixteenth. On the fourteenth, the broadcast announced the surrender to Hitler of the city of Paris. But Paris and its surrender seemed so distant. Near and all-important was the song festival. The next afternoon Mamina and the girls said good-bye to Ruta and Dzintra.

As usual, Uncle Imants was away at the coast. But

the apartment he shared with Vecmamina was crowded that night with the four Darzins from the country. Mamina said they must prepare for early rising by going promptly to bed. Astra declared, "I'm sure I shall not sleep a wink in the noisy city."

Yet it seemed only a moment until she was saying, "Can it be morning so soon?" There was a whirl of dressing and eating breakfast. At the railroad station Astra again cried out in astonishment, "Is *everyone* in Riga going to the song festival?" The excursion train was packed. Above its rumble the Latvian *s's* and *z's* and humming *n's* sounded like bees swarming. The Darzins sisters caught snatches of disturbing talk, of war spreading across continents . . . "I read in the newspaper." . . . "I heard by radio" . . . "Two weeks ago President Ulmanis warned that we may expect hard times, but he declared he had faith in Latvia's strength."

Marga and Astra sought comfort in the passing views. The railroad tracks ran parallel to the river, broad and placid at the capital, but now flowing swiftly through a narrower channel. Log rafts were frequent, floating down to lumber yards or loading wharves at Riga.

At every village station more people squeezed into the crowded coaches. On again, and the girls saw churning white water and the towers of an electric power station. Here was a lofty crag crowned with medieval castle ruins. Bridges were hung with wicker baskets to snare the eel-like lampreys. Now the travelers had entered the province of Latgale, its long valleys studded with lakes which shone blue under open sky, or lay deeply dark in the shadow of forests. The sisters could not have said, perhaps, that the panorama seemed beautiful to them because it was their own country. But they knew it was beautiful with the immemorial charm of summer.

"Why does the world have wars?" Marga turned a troubled face to her father.

"Greater minds than ours have puzzled over that question," he answered. "Men call themselves civilized, yet they battle with one another as in barbaric times."

"I am thinking," mused Mamina, "that perhaps war may be likened to the game which Astra plays at school, the devils beating down a nation's doors with their insane guns and bombshells. *Jā*, even while we watch, they take from us life's loveliest colors—peace, brotherhood, freedom."

The train pulled into the station. "Daugavpils! Daugavpils!" The city's old name, *Castle-on-the-river*, echoed through the coach. Hastily Marga and Astra adjusted their crowns. They stood up, smoothing their embroidered skirts. They fluffed out their snowy sleeves. Although the shadow of fear and anxiety hung over everyone, courage and comradeship suddenly shone bright. "I feel a togetherness with all these people, although I do not know their names," whispered Marga. Astra nodded with understanding. Even if the foe were at the borders of this very province, today there would be brave and glorious song. The tradition of the national singing festival would not be broken.

8 THE FESTIVAL

Edvarts Darzins' business had taken him to many towns. He was well-acquainted with Daugavpils. Beneath the flutter of crimson-and-white banners, and through crowded streets, Edvarts guided his family. He had been withholding a surprise. "My friends Konrads and Aina Ekis have invited us to dinner," he announced. "Here is the shop where they sell musical instruments, and Konrads himself waiting to welcome us. . . . *Labrit,* Konrads my friend, it is so good to see you!"

Mamina was also acquainted with Konrads. There was a sparkle of quick talk and laughter. Marga and Astra were introduced. But their curious glances would stray to the violins and harmoniums, the flutes, trumpets and accordions. On such a festive day it might not have been too surprising had the instruments suddenly united in a resounding *do-re-mi*.

But Konrads quickly ushered his guests through a door at the back of his shop. A corridor led to the family living quarters. It was in the pleasant kitchen that the Darzins presently sat down with their hosts to a meal so joyous and abundant that it was like a Christmas feast. "Anxious talk shall not spoil the good food prepared by my wife," declared Konrads.

Aina blushed scarlet, so that everyone burst out laughing. Laughter became the keynote of the feast. And while Marga and Astra ate with relish, it was Karina Ekis who made the hour memorable for them. Their eyes kept turning to this only child of Konrads and Aina. True, she was just another girl. But she was excitingly new to them, a part of the unusual day in a strange city and a strange room. Moreover, she was pleasant to look at. Her dark braids were intertwined with a blue ribbon and wound around her head. Her voice, both gay and gentle, had surely been tuned to the notes of flute and violin in her father's music shop. And when she said, "I am twelve," and therefore of an age congenial to both Darzins girls, a happy comradeship warmed their hearts.

The table was cleared and the crumbs brushed. Tevs said that surely time might be spared for the Darzins to hear Karina play one selection on her violin. She did so, charming in her Latgallian costume. Then the shop was locked up. All set forth. When the crowds allowed them to go three abreast, Karina walked between Marga and Astra.

"Daugavpils plays fine host today." The Darzins knew that Edvarts' compliment was a matter of courtesy. For they were accustomed to Riga's magnificence, and felt disappointed in Daugavpils. Yet the parks were at their summer loveliest, and the streets flushed clean. Some of the shop windows held still-life groupings of the choicest flowers and jewelry, of hand-carved woods and leathers. Near the esplanade reserved for the festival, shelters had been erected to house exhibits. The people fell into line to view objects recently excavated from ancient castle mounds. There were silver bars used as money in the long ago, and thin, eroded coins in silver and gold. Edvarts and Konrads liked the metal figure of a Viking trader, bearded and booted and skirted, his goods on his back and one hand outstretched in the persuasion of barter. And Mamina cried out, "Just see this antique belt, interwoven with bronze threads in such intricate design! Think of a textile lasting for such hundreds of years!"

"I wonder who wore the girdle in that faraway time," mused Marga, fascinated.

"Some tall, fair woman with long, golden braids who looked like Laima, the Latvian pagan goddess of health and happiness," answered Mamina, smiling. "But now," she said, "it is time for Aina and me to join the choir."

Presently the three girls were seated with their fathers amid the crowd now rapidly filling the bleachers built at one end of the esplanade. "I feel myself trembling in here," confessed Marga, her hand over her heart. There were three empty seats on her right. And now, to the complete surprise of the girls, Cousin Eriks and the Baltais grandparents mounted the steps and took possession of those seats. Such a delighted tumble of questions! "Did you plan all the time to come, and you kept it from us? Did you know we could sit together?"

Edvarts explained how he had arranged that his friend Konrads should buy the tickets in Daugavpils and mail them to Grandfather. "Now everything is perfectly perfect," declared Marga, pressing her cheek against her grandmother's arm.

Astra leaned forward, so happy she could not be less than reckless with compliments. "In all this grandstand, up and down and across," she declared, "there is not a lovelier grandmother." When Grandmother laughed and whispered a warning "Sh-hh!"—Astra added, "Mamina has always said the Kurzeme costume is the prettiest of all the provinces." She turned proudly to Karina. "You have noticed my grandmother's *sakta*?"

"Its amber settings are as fine as any I've seen," agreed Karina.

"The *sakta* is to belong to my baby sister some day, because her name is Dzintra."

But there was no time left for conversation. The Army musicians now appeared in their green uniforms, and marching to their own tunes, mounted the great stage. The procession of singers followed, walking four abreast. First came the women, carrying flowers. The summer sunlight made brighter their gay head scarves and beaded crowns. It glinted on the silver and jewels of their *saktas*. It made rainbows of their colored vests and

billowing skirts. Behind marched the men singers, in
their white shirts and fawn-colored trousers, their skirted,
sleeveless coats, and the embroidered belts that hung
knotted from their waists.

"The great gathering-together of Latvia's festal choirs
always has grandeur for me," murmured Grandfather.

At last the choralists stood ready and waiting. The
audience rose to its feet. The conductor took his place.
He raised his baton, and held it in a tense stillness. It
swung down. Then how the full heart ached to bursting,
how the soul soared to heaven's very gates as the silver-
toned voice of the throng pealed out the prayer for
Latvia:

> "Bless Latvia, O God,
>   Our verdant native sod,
>   Where Baltic heroes trod,
>   Keep her from harm.
>   Our blooming daughters near,
>   Our singing sons appear,
>   May fortune smiling here,
>   Grace Latvia."

"Now our president will speak," whispered Grandfather, wiping his eyes without shame.

But it was only by radio that the President spoke. The
national situation was so grave that he had been obliged
to remain at his palace in Riga. He had asked the
Army's Commander-in-Chief to inform the audience of
the latest developments. "God bless you," the President
concluded, "and all the Latvian people, now and in the
days to come." *The days to come* . . .

The Commander wasted no words. Neither was there any way of softening the dreadful news. "Russia claims that our border guards have attacked some of her soldiers. This proves to the Soviets," said the Commander, grimly sarcastic, "that all of Latvia is intensely hostile. Not only Latvia, but the other Baltic states are accused of having plotted secretly against Russia. Therefore, the Russians declare we have failed to fulfill the mutual-assistance pact made with them last year. So the Red Army demands immediate entry into the Baltic countries, in order 'to make *safe* the formation of new governments.' If we refuse, our cities may expect bombardment. Countrymen, that is all," finished the Commander. "I must now return to the barracks. Attention, all soldiers! Hasten at once to your posts."

The people sat silent and stunned. Grief, anger and despair were written on every face. Yet hope was there, too. Surely the other nations would not stand for Russia's trumped-up excuses for such ruthless invasion of the Baltics.

The choirmaster sprang to the podium. The choir sang "Way to the Native Land," "The Castle of Light," "At the Baltic Sea." The people, listening, wept and yet were comforted.

The Commander's aide came forward to announce and read a telegram from Riga. "Latvia has accepted the terms of Russia's ultimatum!" How else—Latvia so small, so weak in arms and men as compared with Russia's strength, with Russia's long and secret preparations?

Once more the hymn was sung. The crowd broke up, streaming in haste toward trains and buses. Aina Ekis

and Mamina hurried from the stage to join their families. They embraced silently. When he could control his
voice, Grandfather said, "Our enemy has exactly timed
the moment of invasion. Not only is Germany completely
occupied with fighting elsewhere in the world war, but
the Soviets know they must take over the Baltics before
Hitler becomes all-powerful in Europe."

No one could say a word. Eriks was white with anger.
All his high hopes and aspirations seemed crushed. At
the gates of the festival grounds brief farewells were
spoken. For Marga and Astra and Karina it might have
been a parting full of the gay promise of a new friendship. Instead, they could only force their trembling lips
to smile.

Thus the singing festival of 1940 ended. Quickly the
city of Daugavpils was emptied of its guests and its fluttering flags. The homeward journeys were made, to the
north, to the east, to the west.

In the following days Red Army troops arrived in
Riga. A ship brought the ready, loud-mouthed agitators.
Daily, Soviet power was exhibited in processions of
booted feet. From the turrets of rumbling tanks hel-
meted heads lifted, grim as iron. Stores and factories
were roped off and entrance forbidden except by permission of Russian guards. Latvian Communists were
released from prison. Others came out of hiding to join
their Russian comrades. The secret police began weaving its terrible web.

On July twenty-first, President Ulmanis disappeared
from his Riga residence. Never again was he seen by his
countrymen. Never again did he stand before them, and

with affectionate eloquence, address them as *mana tauta*
—"my people." Falsified elections were held. By early
August, Russia announced to the world that Latvia, Lithuania, and Estonia had *begged* to be admitted into the
Soviet Union. "We ask for the right to join the family of
the U.S.S.R." Consent to this plea was proclaimed by the
Russians and celebrated in Moscow with great rejoicing.
To the Baltic peoples they sent their greetings across the
borders in thundering mockery. "We welcome you with
open arms." . . . "Our hearty greetings to you, dear
brothers."

9   SINGING IN THE ORCHARD

Marga was in her fourteenth year that summer of 1941. She had grown tall. She could not help feeling a small, secret joy when her mirror told her she was lovely. "Every day Marga grows more like my own mother," declared Mamina, with open pleasure. How Marga cherished the compliment! Vecmamina Darzins was a dear, kindly little granny, but to Marga her grandmother Baltais seemed to typify Latvian womanhood at its finest, almost as if she were a sculpture or painted symbol. Indeed, when Marga had been but seven years old, she had gazed with awe at the lofty figure upholding the ring of stars atop the Monument of Liberty in Riga. And she had asked her father, "Is the great woman meant to look like my grandmother Baltais?"

On a day that was unusually warm for May, Marga lay in the farm orchard. On the same blanket slept Dzintra, her lashes golden on her cheeks. Astra slumbered under the apple tree she claimed for her own. Propped against another tree, Ruta dozed, her head lolling like that of a rag *lellite*. This hour which followed the noon meal was a time for rest. And in any previous Maytime within Marga's memory, when work hours were many because daylight lasted so long, Mamina might have been resting with her daughters in this narrow paradise of peace. But for a year, now, with the Red Army and its spies in possession of the country, some one on the farm must always be awake and on guard.

Marga moved, uneasily. She was weary from the morning's work, yet she could not sleep. The same sorrows and fears which at night gave her bad dreams, now haunted her. She lifted her book of folk songs and pressed it to her heart, as if the magic it held for her might bring consolation. And the sky, gleaming through the apple boughs, was it not as blue as in happier Maytimes? As in other May days, the orchard was sweet with apple bloom. The ancient and beloved folk songs; sky, sun, and rain; flowers, bees among the blossoms; the mother stork brooding her eggs; rivers and forests and hills—all were the same. Only now the Baltic lands, even the bordering seas, had been taken "under the protection" of the Soviets. This orchard belonged to Tevs and Mamina no more, nor did the house and farm. Mamina was allowed to act only as manager. Tevs' shop with its tools and equipment was only a memory. He and other artisans of Riga were now "employed" by the Communists. The work of their hands was shipped to Russia.

Marga's nervous fingers picked at the edges of her notebook. The Communists could not erase the traditional songs from the loyal heart. But no one dared to sing them aloud. There were no choir rehearsals, no festivals. One could be terribly punished for singing the national anthem. Under cover of darkness last year some unknown citizens had managed to rip down one of the huge portraits of Stalin which confronted Riga day after day. In place of the portrait a Latvian flag glowed in the early light of that Independence Day anniversary. For this crime, the Reds had shot nearly five hundred people. A Latvian dared to be a patriot only within the locked heart, behind locked lips. Outwardly one must be a contented member of "the Soviet family," or suffer. "Suffering beyond tears"— Marga remembered history, and her beloved history teacher.

Only ten nights ago, during the final week of school, while the children slept unaware in the dormitories, the Communists had arrested *kungs* Virzanis. What had been his dreadful fate? And before that, on Easter Sunday, while families worshiped in the parish church, they heard the tramp of heavy boots, and a bull voice shouting, "Pastor, or so you call yourself! You are under arrest as an enemy of the people!" So the pastor was gone. The church was closed. There were no more Christian Sundays.

Marga jerked herself to a sitting position, suddenly so desperately angry that she beat her fists against her knees. She had seen as clearly as anyone the Communist plan of doing away with those who guided Latvia's progress, culture and safety, the teachers and writers and pastors, the army and government officials. They had vanished by the thousands. "Save my dear Grandfather Baltais," prayed Marga in anguish.

She remembered the day the two Communist spies had burst into the Darzins' farmhouse. "Hand over the Latvian flag you are hiding. . . . Where is the news sheet which circulates secretly among you natives?" The spies searched everywhere. They found no newspaper, for there was not a copy on the farm. They found no flag. Only Mamina knew where its crimson folds lay hidden in deep darkness.

That very day the same men had shot young Valdis Bracs. They laid him dead at his father's feet, declaring that he had spied on them from the trees surrounding the Bracs' farmhouse.

And there was Elza Kruze, who had been Valdis' sweetheart, and who had paired so gaily with Cousin Eriks in the Easter swing. One day Elza failed to return from an errand in the village. A month later, at dusk, her young brother Rolands found her on the family doorstep. After that, the neighbors whispered that Elza had surely been a captive of the Russian secret police. Whatever had befallen her, the life and laughter of the old Elza had vanished. She was like a ghost maiden, dull and lost. Often, in the midst of some simple household task, she would stop, not knowing how to go on, not even knowing where she was. Then some terrible memory sent her, crying and trembling, to hide herself.

"God, help poor Elza. Help us all," prayed Marga. "Send
the just and freedom-loving nations to drive the Soviets
out of our land." Tears fell through Marga's fingers.
Then Astra was awake and at her side.

"You have not slept," Astra whispered, anxiously. "You
should try. You are getting so thin. There are dark
shadows under your eyes." Astra leaned forward and
shared a secret. "I heard Mamina tell Tevs that a change
might do you good. She said, 'Perhaps you had better
take Marga to the Baltais farm for a few weeks.' Would
you like that, Marga *milumin?*"

Marga drew her hand across her wet cheeks. "I'm not
sure," she answered. "I love the big Baltais farm. I have
not seen Grandmother since the song festival in Daugavpils last year. Often and often I long for her. But Mamina needs me here. And what if something should
happen to any of you while I am away? Oh, sister, I am
ashamed you saw me cry! I wish I could be brave, and
sleep and forget, as you do."

"I do not forget," answered Astra, gently. "But I can
sleep. Perhaps it is because I am only eleven."

"I wish I could be brave like Mamina and Tevs,"
mourned Marga, unable to stop. "When Tevs leaves for
Riga each Monday, they never say that he may not come
home again. When Mamina takes our weekly quota of
produce to the Communist collection center in the village, she says never a word, although she knows that the
freight cars will pack it off to Russia. Mamina never
mentions how the freights come back empty, but chalked
in huge letters, FOR STARVING LATVIA, as if they
were stuffed with wonderful things. Astra! How can

the Communists believe they are really fooling us?"
Marga choked, then went on feverishly.

"But maybe they do fool our first-graders, who read in
their new Russian primers that 'all children love Josef
Stalin with untold love.' But except for the fanatical
young Communist Pioneers, they do not fool us older
pupils. Yet with what devotion must we write essays
about 'our great father!' We stuff albums full of his pho-
tographs. We sing and recite in honor of his glorious
birthday." Marga's voice rose in hysteria. She fought
for self-control. "Oh, Astra," she moaned, "when we had
our freedom, it was so easy for me to write in my notebook that no matter what happened, I would sing as our
ancestors sang in their own deep trouble. But now I am
not brave enough to sing."

"None of us can sing as we used to—not loud," answered Astra. "But let's you and me sing in a whisper,
here in the orchard." To please Marga, Astra thumbed
through the notebook. "I like this one. It is a bride, singing." Blond heads close, the sisters sang very softly:

> "Carry back to mother dear
> A hundred greetings.
> Thank her for the way she combed my hair,
> And for the shoes upon my feet."

"Such a sweet song," reflected Marga, "yet sad, as
if the maiden were already hungry for home. This
song is sad, too, but it makes a picture in my mind." All
at once, pale with resolve, Marga sprang to her feet. Her

voice, high and clear, soared up through the apple boughs:

"I was a fine songstress,
  Like a bluebird on a branch.
  They gave me to strangers
  Where no songs were heard."

Marga dropped to the rug again, suddenly full of youthful merriment. "There!" she cried. "Singing at the top of my voice has made me feel new and strong! Astra, I'm sure that 'place where no songs are heard' must be Siberia."

"Don't talk about Siberia," whispered Astra. "There's Mamina at the kitchen door, her eyes full of questions because you sang. And now Dzintra is awake. Isn't she the prettiest *lellite* in all Vidzeme?"

"She will be three in November. She has learned to say almost everything." Marga bent to kiss the little sister.

Both girls were startled when Tonis suddenly scrambled to his feet, his neck hairs bristling, his barks furious. Ruta woke up, and was about to stand when she thought better of it. This past year one had learned to freeze the body into stillness, when necessary, to freeze the face until there was not so much the flicker of an eyelash. And now it seemed necessary. For a bicycle was wheeling up the lane. A man alighted. With strong but deliberate steps he strode toward the orchard. Marga slipped her notebook under the rug. Mamina came quietly from the house. Calling out a quick command to

Tonis, she clutched and held him by the scruff of his
neck.

"I am an inspector from the regional Communist
headquarters," the newcomer announced, pompously.

"I remember you well, *kungs* Kangars," answered Mamina. "Formerly you kept a sausage booth in the village
market house." If Mamina's voice was edged with scorn,
her manner was polite. And even though Kangars was
a Latvian turned traitor, did not Mamina's use of the title
kungs sound highly respectful?

"Never mind," snapped Kangars. "I now work under
the Red Star." He cleared his throat. "The one who preceded me in office was too easy on you peasants. In fact,
so easy that he himself is now taking life easy in a Si-
berian labor camp." Kangars' teeth gleamed in evil
amusement. He thumbed through a packet of cards.
"For instance," he continued, "if a farm-wife had written
on her declaration card that she had a flock of thirty
chickens, but was in reality hiding four more in the cellar, my predecessor was not likely to search the cellar. If
she declared four cows, but in her deceit hid a fifth one
in the forest, did my predecessor investigate? Not as I
do! I, Kangars the inspector, search the cellars. I set
spies to watch the carrying of the milk to and from the
forest. Today I check the honesty of the peasants in my
district. I see by this card that you declare the manage-
ment of forty chickens."

"Since the last declaration," answered Mamina, crisply,
"we have cooked and eaten two hens. Another is at present on a setting of eggs. Within a few days, therefore,
the flock may be enlarged by eight or nine."

"All to be shared with the people." The inspector's pious quotation was needled with ice. "This card also declares that you manage five cows."

"You may count them in yonder field. I have none concealed in the forest, in the cellar, nor under the beds." Mamina's mouth twitched ever so slightly.

"We shall see about that," Kangars mocked. "But first —" his smile was wicked—"it was refreshing, as I wheeled up, to hear music. For on my rounds among the peasants today I have met with nothing but long faces, and heard only glum mutterings. But on this farm I find happiness so great that the daughters sing loud and clear. Their father Stalin, who loves all children, would rejoice to know that here they dwell content under the generous Stalinist sun." The inspector's glance flicked over Ruta, Marga and Astra. "Perhaps one of you was singing the Communist hymn. If so, what a pity to waste it on the apple blossoms! Won't you sing it again for me?"

"We would sing it for you," spoke up Ruta, her voice as smooth as butter, "but we do not know the tune."

"Ah-hh," breathed the inspector, his eyes glittering, "in time our Communist song of a better world for all will be the only tune you know. Nothing native to poor old-time Latvia can be so inspiring as the Russian-born 'Arise, ye prisoners of starvation; arise, ye wretched of the earth.' However, this orchard is a very pleasant place, and I am tired. You will sing for me, now, whatever song you please." Leaning idly against a tree, Kangars folded his arms and waited.

Astra hid her trembling lips against Dzintra's curls. Under her apron Ruta clenched her fists. Marga searched

her mother's face, now white and strained. Then the
girl, who but a moment ago had wept because she was
not brave, stood up, bravely. She turned to Kangars, her
young beauty pale, yet radiant. "It was I who sang as
you arrived, Inspector," she said. "And now I will sing
for you a song of the dear country in which you and I
live, and of its trees which our ancestors worshiped:

> "Sunlight in the evening scatters
> Gifts upon the forest treetops:
>
> Golden crown upon the linden,
> Silver crown upon the oak,
>
> Leaves of diamond on the birch tree,
> Golden rings upon the willow."

"You who were born Latvian, does not your heart re-
call that beautiful song?" Marga's eyes asked it of the
man with the folded arms. But he only answered with a
steady, black-browed gaze. The orchard was silent except for the droning of the bees. All the pale faces were
turned toward the inspector. Suddenly he shook himself. He straightened, and barked out, "I am Kangars
the inspector. I inspect barns, sheds, *klets, pirts*. I inspect house from cellar to loft. Call in your cows, that I
may inspect them."

"There is a horse and plow to inspect, and the man
plowing the field," suggested Mamina, pointing to Mikelis.

"Let them be," growled Kangars. With fine Commu-
nistic courtesy he preceded Mamina into the house.

Before following him she spoke to Ruta, "Take Dzintra with you when you bring in the cows." And with secret gestures, Mamina made known to the girls that they must inform Mikelis of what was going on. She could see him, in his alarmed curiosity, making very uneven furrows in the brown earth.

On the way to the meadow Astra slipped her arm around Marga. "Sister, you are as brave as anyone can be."

"Jā, brave to the point of danger," declared Ruta, wiping her eyes on her apron. "The sight of her singing for that devil I shall never forget. And if I had them, I would bet a pocketful of *lats* that neither can he forget."

"Oh, Ruta!" cried Marga. "Will he send our cows to Russia? We love them! They are ours!"

"Sh-hh! Under the Communists we own nothing. The Soviet state owns everything, even our bodies and souls," Ruta jerked her thumb backward, in contempt of Kangars.

"Go slowly, Ruta, while I tell Mikelis. He is popeyed with questions." Astra sped across the fields.

"It's a new inspector from the village," she told the hired man. "Only I think he must be the devil himself, or one of the historic German Black Knights who has risen in evil out of the black earth. God in heaven," prayed Astra, right there in the field, "don't let the devil take away our cows, especially dear Brune."

Mikelis stared at her blankly. Then, turning his back to the house in case the inspector might be spying, Mikelis made a most terrible face. At any other time, it would have been funny.

Presently the three girls were driving the herd back to the cattle yard. Their faces had no more expression than masks.

"Now that you are no longer allowed to line your pockets with *lats* from the sale of milk and cheese," announced Kangars, "five cows to supply a family of six proclaims high living indeed. There are others less fortunate who will welcome your cows. Tomorrow you will bring two of them to the collecting center in the village. Which three of these animals are the best?"

Mamina laid her hand upon Brune, upon Margrietina, upon Madam.

"I know that trick," answered Kangars, triumphantly. "A peasant wife will always declare her poorest to be her best. You may keep these three poorest on which you have laid your hand." And jotting down a reminder on the card he held, the inspector jovially pinched Dzintra's cheek, strode toward his bicycle, mounted it and rode off.

The group in the cattle yard stood rooted, more still than trees. But when Kangars had dwindled to a moving speck on the road, Ruta muttered from between clenched teeth, "I hurry to wash the print of dirty fingers from our baby's innocent cheek."

Marga and Astra, leaning fondly against the cows, began to cry. But Mamina scolded them gently. "*Nē!* Let not one tear fall! Others in our land weep for sons and daughters, for husbands and wives and grandparents, killed or taken away by the Communists. Who are we, together and whole, to weep for the loss of our animals, dear and useful as they are to us?" Mamina managed a grim chuckle. "And in spite of Kangars' suspicions, we do keep our best, Brune, Margrietina, Madam. Return the cows to pasture, Ruta. Daughters, get to your weeding. *Work*—how it helps the aching and angry heart!"

After the girls had begun the weeding, Astra made an excuse to run to the house again. She whispered to her mother. "Is Marga to go to the Baltais farm?"

Mamina's answer was troubled. "Your sister's sorrow for the Latvian people has been greatly intensified because she sees, near at hand, what can happen to one person. I mean poor Elza Kruse. Marga broods over Elza in pity and horror. If a visit to the grandparents could be safely made, the change of scene might help our Marga." Mamina gave herself a little shake. "But there, *milumin!* It is a lovely day. And when you and Marga are tired from weeding, come in for some fresh sugared bread and apple-blossom tea."

There are
my Songs

10   BEYOND TEARS

Mikelis was a pony. Dzintra, on his shoulder, was a bouncing little rider, not caring that he cavorted so awkwardly. Even Astra, walking by Mikelis' side as they brought the cows in from pasture, was surprised that her little sister's high-riding glee could bring to her own lips a smile, the first, surely, since the dreadful word had come about Marga.

Mikelis lived at the Darzins' place all the time, now. It was safer for him than in the village. Besides, he was no longer needed to help the widow Kruze. She and her son Rolands had left the neighborhood for Riga. How thankful the Darzins were to have the good Mikelis, both for his help and his company, but mostly because he devoted himself to guarding the small-girl happiness natural to Dzintra. If he were around when Ruta's tears dropped into the soup kettle, or when Edvarts fell into one of his haggard silences, Mikelis would whisk Dzintra away for an hour of odd, peasant-born story-telling which none of the family had ever dreamed he could offer. Perhaps Mikelis himself was surprised.

Now, on this July evening, Mamina came to do the milking. A fresh pain smote Astra on seeing her mother so thin and white, walking as if in illness, yet so brave and composed. Mikelis reached to take the empty pails from her, but she shook her head. "Nē, Mikelis, this everyday chore in the peace of the evening is strangely healing to me."

She went on, more briskly. "You have worked hard today, Mikelis. Wash and rest yourself. Supper will be later than usual, for Edvarts will be arriving by the second bus. Astra, take Dzintra with you and pull some greens for the rabbits. We must treat them well. Their brothers were food for us when the Communists were taking our eggs and chickens." Mamina gazed tenderly at Dzintra. "Every day," she murmured, "the child grows more like our Marga."

Astra ran to press her cheek against her mother's arm. For a moment she struggled against the terrible ache in her throat. "Oh, Mamina, I am glad that you say Marga's name again."

"In the long night," answered her mother, "it came to me that we must be brave enough to say it often and easily. To say *Marga* brings her back to us as she was, and shall always be, in our hearts."

"But Tevs won't—"

"The courage to speak of Marga by name will come to him later, I hope," said Mamina. She motioned Mikelis to take Dzintra into the house. Lowering herself to a log which had been dragged in from the woods for chopping, she drew Astra down beside her. "The cows and the rabbits can wait a few moments," she said. "I have strengthened myself to talk to you, my daughter. Together we must face this tragedy which has come to us. You will soon be twelve. I want you to understand the part your father and I had in it."

"You know, daughter, how Marga longed to visit the Baltais farm. There was the novelty of travel in the midst of the sad, dreary days, and the joy of reunion with those she loved, especially with her grandmother. *Jā*, we knew it might be dangerous, but have we not lived with danger every hour? We could only trust we had done the right thing for Marga. But in the night our Tevs cries out, 'Why was I such a fool not to realize, since her grandfather held high office in his country, that he would surely be deported? Why did not God stretch forth His hand and stop me from taking her there? . . . If only I had never bought the train ticket! . . . If only . . .'

"So your father will not say Marga's name, nor hear it. He turns away in heartsickness from the sight of her belongings. But we know he is grim and bitter because he suffers so. We must try to help him think of Marga as still with us."

"If only the pastor were here to help him," murmured Astra.

"And to help us all," agreed her mother. "But I think a moment may come when Tevs will listen to you. Watch for that moment. You are a great comfort. You have grown old in sad wisdom."

"Mamina," faltered Astra, feeling, on the contrary, young and confused, "I have longed to ask, yet I was afraid. . . . Forgive me, Mamina, but do you think that Marga is—is alive somewhere?"

"Of course we do not know. But I—I hope . . . I mean it would be better if Marga had died, and quickly." Mamina covered her face with her hands. Astra's embracing arm felt how rigid her mother sat, holding back her racking grief. After a hard moment, she gained control of herself.

The cows were lowing. As Mamina reached for the pails, Astra begged, "One thing more, please, Mamina. In the nights I wonder about Eriks. . . ."

"I never cease wondering. The Germans, who are our masters since they drove out the Russians last month, are now drafting our young men into their army, although it is only fair to say that many Latvians are enlisting willingly, hoping to save our country from another Soviet invasion. We do not know whether Eriks would be one to enlist, or to dodge the draft. Should he be alive and in hiding, we must not endanger him by trying to learn his whereabouts." Mamina got to her feet. "Now, as you and Dzintra gather the greens, keep watch for your father. He should be here presently."

Dzintra's fingers were not kind to the lettuce plants,

for she pulled them up by the roots. She soon tired of it.
Pointing to the storks, she began waving her arms up
and down. "Dzintra will fly some day," she declared.

"*Nē,*" protested Astra. "You must stay at home with
me."

"*Jā,*" agreed Dzintra, "because now I sleep where
Marga did, in the big bed with you." The child put her
finger to her lip. "Sh-hhh! It is Tevs!"

How astonishing, thought Astra, that little Dzintra
also realized that no one dare mention Marga within her
father's hearing! Hastening to scatter the greens in the
rabbits' pen, Astra took Dzintra's hand. "*Lellite,* when
you are older, I will tell you all about our dear Marga. I
will teach you her favorite songs. But now let's give Tevs
our bravest smiles and tightest hugs."

"What is 'bravest?' " asked Dzintra, riding to the house
in her father's arms.

" 'Bravest' is your mamina, Janiti," he murmured.
" 'Brave' is your sister. Where is your mother?" he demanded anxiously of Astra.

"She is milking the cows." Astra smiled at him.

"I will get on my work clothes," he said.

Suddenly it occurred to Astra that the milking had
been going on too long. The times made her easily
alarmed. She sped swiftly to the cow stables. At the
door she paused, dizzy with mingled fright, astonishment, and joy.

Mamina was lying on the earthen floor. Her milking
stool and pail were overturned, and the spilled milk had
darkened the straw under Brune's feet. Kneeling by
Mamina, chafing her wrists, was . . .

"Cousin Eriks!" cried Astra. "When—what has happened to my mother?"

"I tried not to startle her," answered Eriks. "First I called a warning from the hay where I have been sleeping since dawn. When I came to her, she had fallen in a faint. But look, cousin, she opens her eyes!"

Mamina's eyelids fluttered. Then her gaze was upon Eriks, slowly gathering full knowledge of him. "Did anyone—*anyone*—come with you?" she whispered. Eriks shook his head, sadly. The hope which had brightened Mamina's face went out like a light. No one with Eriks. But Eriks himself—*jā*. Astra flew to the house.

"Tevs! Eriks is here. Eriks is with Mamina!"

That same white hope blazed in Tevs' eyes. "Did Eriks bring—"

"*Nē*, Tevs! Cousin Eriks came alone. He says that he walked all the way from the Baltais farm. He was so weary he's been sleeping in the hay for hours. Mamina fainted when he called to her."

Astra was obliged to jump aside as her father rushed from the house. In his absence, she could cry for a moment in Ruta's arms. "But it will never do." She braced herself. "Come, *lellite!*" she cried pretending to be gay for Dzintra's sake. "Let me make you pretty for Cousin Eriks. Ruta, we must set a place for him. He looks very thin and hungry. And Mamina will need that hot soup you have made."

Vigorously Ruta stirred the soup. "*Jā*," she agreed, brokenly, "the good soup for the good *kundze*."

At the supper table, Dzintra must sit close to Eriks. She was too young to remember him, but she knew he was worthy of her charms even though he was so pale and unshaven. She turned on him her most trusting gaze. She offered him a kiss flavored with bread crumbs and soup. Eriks was enchanted. He lifted her bright ringlets. "Amber girl, how much you look like—" He stopped, noting Astra's sidelong warning glance. After a moment, he began again.

"Amber—that reminds me. Last year, after the singing festival at Daugavpils, Grandmother placed her *sakta* in a cotton-lined box. She said to me, 'With the Red Army and the secret police among us, we put away our festival ornaments as we put away our happiness. If anything befalls me, Eriks, you must take this *sakta* to my granddaughter Dzintra. I pledged it to her.' Grandmother then told me the hiding place she had chosen for the brooch. But you see"—Eriks frowned, pondering—"so much has happened, and I cannot now remember. I have searched in all the likely places, but in vain.

"I was with my great-aunt and uncle in Kurzeme when Mar—when my cousin came to the farm," Eriks went on. "So I missed her visit. I was still away when on those terrible nights of June the thirteenth and fourteenth the Communists raided thousands of homes and killed or deported so many of the Baltic people, among them our—our own. When we heard of it, great-aunt would not let me leave, but one night I slipped away in secret. I must know what had happened at the Baltais farm.

"When I arrived there, I hid myself for a first view. The house seemed the same, but desolate. The forge was partly burned. The big flour mill lay in ashes, and the beautiful orchard stood blackened, for of course it was the Russian aim to leave as little as possible for the advancing German troops.

"Grandfather's permanent farm hands were still there, looking after the fields and animals. But they were feeble with shock. The few summer workers had fled, having first helped themselves to food, and to linens and blankets from Grandmother's weaving room. I'm wondering if they found and took her *sakta*."

Eriks closed his eyes. His voice shook. "Aunt, uncle, cousin, I shall not repeat to you what the farm hands told me of that dreadful night. *Nē*, I cannot speak of it yet. But they said the courage of our people was a thing beyond belief."

Eriks paced the floor. "What a fool I was to cherish a dream of planting and reaping in peace for my own prosperity and that of my country!" he blurted out, his voice rough. "Would that forty thousand like me might have been in Riga the day the Russians left, when our patriots seized the radio stations and public buildings and proclaimed Latvia free. Alas, the patriots were too few! The moment was too short!

"Now the Nazis call themselves our liberators. Now they claim the Baltic nations as their rightful inheritance. They give us a new name—Ostland. It is to be new living space for them. Oh, *jā*, they do allow us to sing our national hymn. They have allowed us to open our churches again. But let me tell you, Uncle Edvarts, there is a fun-making song which some Latvians now sing in secret. It goes something like this: 'The people cheer with full delight. A robber has freed us from a robber's might.' *Jā*, do you get that?

"And I will tell you. If we suffer again under the Nazis, I shall take to ambush—to the bogs and the forests. With others like me, I shall harass and kill whatever enemy is Latvia's enemy."

"Oh, Eriks, how changed you are!" moaned his aunt.

"Of course!" Eriks' chuckle was not pleasant to hear. "Changed because of what has happened to my grand-parents and cousin, and to—to Elza Kruze, that laugh-ing girl."

Eriks could not say enough. Treading the starlit miles to the Darzins farm, his personal sufferings and those of his country had piled up in his mind. "Do you know," he went on, "how in those last days the Communists set up their machine guns in the windows of the library at Riga, that library begun in the fourteenth century? I have seen those books and priceless manuscripts through which the *Ivans* thrust their bayonets, and the halls they afterward burned to the ground. I have seen the Old City, Riga's very cradle. It is now a mass of rubble."

A groan of protest came from Edvarts. "What good, Eriks, to name these tragedies, one by one? It would take you the rest of your life. Besides, we know them quite as well as you do."

Mamina spoke soothingly. "Mikelis has lighted the wall lantern in the *pirts*. He has kindled the fire. A steam bath will relax us all."

"*Jā*, a bath will be good," Eriks agreed. "I will bring my bundle from the hay."

Returning, Eriks took his personal belongings from

the bundle. Then he spread a colorful mass on the table. "Aunt Kristine," he said, "I knew you would wish to keep this."

"To keep, always," murmured Mamina. She rested her hand on the soft wool of Grandmother Baltais' white shawl, so richly embroidered in the "holy-tree" oak design. There were the familiar bright reds and blacks of the beautiful Kurzeme costume. Suddenly Mamina's hand tightened on the folds. "There is something else here, Eriks?" she asked. "Is it—can it be the box holding the *sakta*?"

"*Nē*, I told you that I cannot find the *sakta*," answered Eriks. "Dear aunt, that which lies under your hand— well, at the Baltais farm, or what is left of it—I said to myself, '*Jā*, I will carry this treasure to the Darzins family, where it belongs. . . . *Nē*,' I argued, 'take it I must not. The sight of it will hurt them too much.' And so it was *jā* one moment, and *nē* the next, and I did not know what was right to do." Troubled and hesitant, Eriks studied the tense faces around him. Then he threw back the shawl.

"Marga's notebook! It is Marga's book of folk songs!" Gladness rang in Astra's voice. But Mamina sank back in her chair, her hands shaking against her cheeks. Ruta burst into tears. Edvarts strode to the open door, his back to the room, while he stared out, unseeing. His voice was thick with grief and anger. "You are a blundering oaf, Eriks Baltais, not to know the suffering this book brings us!"

"Hush, Edvarts, hush! Eriks did the right thing." Mamina turned to her nephew, forcing herself to ask calmly. "You found the book of songs in the farmhouse?"

Eriks delayed the difficult answer. "Shall I tell you? . . . *Jā*, I will, for you would always be wondering. The notebook was found by the Latvian freight agent in the shunting yards at Jelgava. It had been flung from the cattle car in which our dear ones, with many others, had been packed and locked for deportation. I heard about the finding of the book, and I went after it. From the description I felt sure it must be—my cousin's. So it was, but you will see that it is changed. No longer is it merely a girl's fair and innocent treasure. It is a testimony to a nation's pain. For its margins are scrawled with final messages from those poor people in that cattle car, unsigned but—"

"Stop, idiot! I cannot bear another word!" Edvarts Darzins turned. And rushing to the table, he snatched up the book. Then he was outside, hurrying down to the bath-house.

It was partly Mamina's feeble gesture of entreaty which sent Astra flying after her father. She was close on his heels as he stooped to enter the *pirts*. She saw him walk toward the fiery pit that lay beneath the boulders. "Tevs!" she called.

He turned sharply. "Go back to the house!" he commanded. "I will burn this book. It shall not live among our belongings to haunt us with a never-ending sorrow."

Astra was shaking. Yet she steeled herself to speak with calmness. "Tevs, the book is not yours to destroy. It is still Marga's. It is Mamina's. It is mine and Dzintra's, a very precious treasure. Tevs, please?"

Astra was startled at the suddenness with which her

father thrust the book at her, as if he could no longer bear to touch it. She saw him slump to his knees on the earthen floor, his hands over his face. She knelt beside him, her arms warm around his neck.

"Oh, Tevs, don't you see?" she whispered. "The book of folk songs *is* Marga and all that was finest in her—her love of poetry and music, her love for Latvia. We *must* keep it."

The great stones in the *pirts* glowed red hot. The dark walls of the cave were colored a deep, dull red. Astra, struggling against her youth and inexperience, tried to think what more she could say. "Tevs," she began again, bravely, "today Mamina and I had a long talk. We have resolved that from now on we will speak of Marga in a natural way, as if she were here. For if we cannot do that, how can she live on in our hearts and our home? Tevs, we are not being faithful to her if we're always tiptoeing around her name in silence, as if we were afraid of her, as if we didn't love her any more. Tevs, won't you—oh," Astra cried, helplessly, "I wish I were old enough to know the right words. I wish I were our pastor talking to you. But I am only—" she was Tevs' little girl, sobbing in his arms.

"There, there, *milumin*," he murmured. "I have been selfish and hard, locked away in my grief for Marga. *Jā*, daughter, you hear how I say her name." He wiped Astra's cheeks. "Now, could you go to the house? Your mother will be wondering about us. And I was very rough with Eriks. Tell him to join me in the hospitality of the *pirts*. The steam bath will do more than cleanse our bodies."

Spent after the storm of her tears, Astra climbed the

terrace slowly. When almost to the top, she met her mother, saw her hesitate, and knew it was because Mamina was wondering which needed her more, Astra, or Edvarts. But Astra nodded reassuringly, pointing to the notebook.

Once in her room, she opened it, and saw on its margins those pitiful penciled scrawls. "Good-bye." . . . "Save Latvia." . . . "Good-bye, my beloved." . . . "We die for Latvia." . . . "Good-bye." . . . Who had written these words, in agony? Astra felt sickened by the terrible pictures forming in her mind. Swiftly she knelt, pulled out a lower drawer of the chest, and hid the notebook under a pile of folded clothing. "I can never bear to look at it again," she said to herself.

She lay down on her bed, staring at the ceiling. But after a while she got up and took the book from the drawer. She opened it again, trying, without success, to recognize Marga's handwriting among those final farewells. Slowly a strange kind of realization came to her, and with it, a sense of peace. "Why," she whispered, "I need not be afraid of this book! Every song in it, which Marga copied so lovingly, is a message from her. 'Carry back to mother dear a hundred greetings.' . . . 'Thank her.' . . . 'They gave me to strangers.' . . . These are my songs and the songs of my people. As they sang, in sorrow and in joy, so shall I try to sing, no matter what happens."

"No matter what happens . . . Oh, Marga! Marga, my lost sister!"

Astra laid the book of folk songs on the table by the window. A shaft of late golden sunlight struck across it, warmly and familiarly.

11 FLIGHT FROM HOME

"Wait! I'll be quick. Something I remember to do." Tevs' words sounded rusty in the pewter-dark dawn. His daughters, ready to climb into the wagon seat beside Mamina, watched him hurry toward the orchard. His running feet seemed larger than life in the light cast around them by his lantern.

"Wait! I forgot something." Dzintra dashed after her father. Her voice floated behind her like a rippling, fine-spun ribbon. "Only to say good-bye to my apple tree, Mamina."

"Please—" Astra spoke with apology. She was fourteen. Mamina relied on her so much. And last evening,

when two of the German soldiers billeted at the Bracs
farm came to say that the people of the parish had but
a few hours to gather their things together and leave
their homes, Mamina had said to her family that at least
there would be no time this morning for painful farewells. Astra remembered, but . . . "Please, Mamina, only
a little moment . . ."

She, too, then, sped toward the orchard. By that time
Dzintra had finished her own errand and was watching
her father. He was kneeling. His fingers, pink in the
lantern light, made hasty, scooping motions, except when
they paused to push aside Tonis' inquisitive nose. Digging in earth was a thing Tonis understood, not all these
early morning preparations for travel which made a dog
frantic for fear he might be left behind.

Astra hastened to find her tree. She pressed her cheek
against it. "*Sveiki*, dear apple tree," she whispered. "Be
here, the same as ever, when some day we shall come
back." Through the shadows she slipped from trunk to
trunk, and again her cheek found rough bark. "*Sveiki*,
Marga's tree." Her sigh breathed out. Her hands
lingered, caressing. Then she ran to join her father and
sister as they returned to the wagon. She saw the small
tin box in Tevs' hand. On the lid the word Primus,
faintly visible in the lantern light, told her that it was a
container for lamp wicks, commonly bought in the
village.

"Did you, after all, dig up some of our buried treasure?" she asked.

"None that we buried last evening," answered her

father. "But in this small box we shall carry away with
us a bit of our own Latvian earth."

"Oh, Tevs, you sound like *forever!* Please, we *shall*
come back to our farm?"

"That is the hope which sustains us all. *Jā*, surely
some day we come home again."

"Then this morning I shall not feel quite so sad. . . .
Up you go, little sister, into the wagon."

Edvarts blew out the light and set the lantern in the
wagon bed. He came around to lay his hand on Mamina's. "Ready, now. Steady," he said. Mounting his
bicycle, he pedaled slowly through the farm lane.
Mamina gathered up the reins and clucked to Gipsy.
As the horse stepped forward, the load in the wagon
shifted, and the cow Brune, hitched behind, strained
stubbornly against the pull of the rope. But it was too
much for her. She fell into step. Tonis, yelping, raced
first on one side, then on the other. He was in a frenzy
of anxiety.

"Poor old pet!" murmured Mamina. "The moment will
come when he must drop behind."

"Then who will take care of him?" Dzintra quavered.

"Some kind person, we hope." Mamina's voice was
steady. She was tearless. She did not know that Astra
had seen her in heartbreak but an hour ago. For Astra
had crept away from the sight of her mother placing
lavish amounts of food and water here and there in the
yards, then turning out of their shelters the trusting
animals she had loved and tended and now must aban-
don to their fate. The secret tears had streamed down
Mamina's cheeks. Remembering, Astra shivered.

"The morning is chill," Mamina now said, evenly. "Wrap yourself and Dzintra closely in the blanket."

Astra could see the shadowy line of farm wagons waiting on the highway. Her father waited there, also, until Mamina could turn the wagon into the space reserved for her by neighbor Bracs, behind, and in front, the Valters. "Coming, Rudolfs," shouted Edvarts, wheeling to the head of the cavalcade. He and Rudolfs were to guide it along various back roads leading into Riga, for the main highways were choked with German troops and tanks in retreat from the advancing Russians.

For now, in 1944, the tides of war had again turned. At Leningrad, at Paris, in northern Africa and Italy, in the Netherlands and on far-flung Pacific islands, the Allies, of which Russia was one, were victorious. In July the dreaded Soviets, as enemies of the Nazis, had again invaded the Baltic countries. Since then, family after family had fled before them, by day hiding in swamp or forest, or in haylofts of friendly barns. By night, dodging the ever-shifting battle zones, they made their painful way toward the yet free ports of Riga and the Kurzeme coast. Through it all those who survived assured themselves, "The voices of the western nations will soon echo around the world, crying out in the name of justice that our lands be restored to us."

In this September dawn, the moon in the sky was a moon eaten away to smallness, like an old eroded coin. Scarcely risen, it shed only enough light to show the shape of the Darzins' house and outbuildings, the mass of surrounding trees, the faint glimmer of the lake, the ghostly mist over the meadows. "Now we are on the road. We face the future. We shall not look back."

Mamina said it, bravely. But as the wagon lurched forward, it was as if a compelling hand turned her head. Astra's, too. *Oh, home of my heart, good-bye. Good-bye to the sociable family chairs, and the beds in which we have rested from work. Good-bye to the tables still holding our lamps and our books, and the pictures on our walls. Good-bye to the homely things of the kitchen, the dishes, the kettles and pans. To all the treasures of the klets, we say good-bye—the big, kind cupboard and Marga's dowry chest, with their painted designs and the beloved things they hold. Good-bye to the woven and embroidered pieces which were my mother's pride. Good-bye to the family silver we hid in the dark earth, and Dzintra's doll which she sang to sleep and buried with tears. Meadows which have known my running feet, fields in which I have worked, lake which I have loved, when shall I see you again? Flower garden—lilac and peony, rose and brokenheart, bloom for us another spring.*

Jā, jā, memories were about all the Darzins could take away with them. In the wagon bed were two suitcases containing the most necessary clothing. There was grain for Gipsy and Brune, food for the family—smoked and salted meats, zweibach, cheese, honey, jams, some dressed chickens. Last night, when they were all so confused, Mamina had said, "Choose a few keepsakes. In time they may mean more to us than anything."

"I shall take Marga's notebook of folk songs," said

Astra, "my own book of pressed flowers, and the amber nugget I've been saving for Dzintra."

"Before burying our silver, I saved out the knives and forks," Mamina said. "Let us also take the festival shawl which belonged to your grandmother Baltais." Which made Dzintra think of Grandmother's lost *sakta*, and then of Eriks. "If Cousin should come here after we are gone, how can he know where we are?"

The family had not seen Eriks for a year. Gaunt as a wolf, grim as the pistol at his belt, he had come secretly in the night, and had slipped away before dawn. For now Eriks was a member of the guerilla band, the "Freedom Fighters," stealing out with his detachment to derail a train, or to set ablaze a Russian encampment, harassing the Reds continually, shooting from cover, hiding, then moving quickly on to another swamp, another forest.

So good-bye to Eriks. And to Ruta and Mikelis, good-bye. The Darzins had never heard from Ruta since July, when she had hurried off to her native Latgale to urge her mother and young brother to flee the Communists while they could. As for Mikelis, he had sturdily announced his determination to stay in the village. "It is my birthplace. I will take what comes."

But now the conversations and the feverish preparations of the previous night were past. It was the morning of flight. To Riga—but after that?

Shortly before Edvarts and Rudolfs motioned the cavalcade to turn into a side road, a great explosion was heard. A moment later, a high, hysterical sobbing came from the Bracs' wagon, immediately behind. Astra pushed aside the blanket from her cheek, trying to turn far enough to see, but discovered that she was dragging the blanket from Dzintra. Sidewise, however, she glimpsed a fierce, spreading glow in the eastern sky, and presently, tongues of flame licking at the moon.

"Mamina!" It was no more than a terrified sigh. Astra saw how her mother sat erect as a soldier, facing her journey. Had she not heard the explosion and seen the flames? Life seemed to drain from Astra as she had imagined it leaving her body the day she and her school-mates had been obliged to give their blood for the enemy soldiers last spring. Now she longed to shrink smaller and smaller under the blanket, away from sight and sound, away from horror. Then came Dzintra's voice, childish and plaintive. "Is it the *kundze* Bracs who cries? And why?"

Strength flowed back into Astra. She drew Dzintra closer. "Perhaps *kundze* Bracs cries only because she is cold."

"We could give her our blanket," offered Dzintra.

The wailing went on, unbearably. Without turning her head, Mamina called out, "Janis Bracs my friend, my little daughter Dzintra wishes to lend her blanket if the poor *kundze* cries from cold."

"My wife is not cold. Surely you see in the sky, *kundze* Darzins, the cause of her mourning," came Janis' answer.

"*Jā*, I see," answered Mamina. "It is the *kundze's* years of happiness and all her earthly treasures that flame in the sky."

Kundze Bracs cried all the louder.

Again Mamina called out. "Neighbor Janis, my child frets that perhaps the *kundze* cries from hunger. She offers to bring a share of cheese and smoked pork from our wagon."

"My wife is not hungry," answered Janis, "and of food we have enough. *Kundze* Darzins, you are hard."

"Not hard, dear friend," called Mamina, her voice breaking. "But the way is hard for all of us. Shall the piteous wailing of one make it more difficult, especially for our little ones, who are already so sadly confused? *Kundze* Bracs, look to the west. See how the Nazi soldiers reduce to flame and ashes the treasure of others!" Mamina put her left arm around her daughters, holding them so tightly under the blanket they could see neither to right nor left. Was that a sudden terrible sob bursting from Mamina's throat? Or was she only coughing? Could Mamina mean that the Darzins' farm buildings were on fire? *Mamina, don't tell us. Hold us close, Mamina. Hide us.*

Presently *kundze* Bracs ceased her crying. Slowly grew the full light of day, but misty and chill, without sun. The back roads were muddy from the autumn rains, except those leading through the woods where pine needles lay thick. "Good morning, forest mother," murmured Astra, finding sudden childish comfort in the folk rhyme.

"When I was very small," said Mamina, "there was World War One. With my brother, who became Eriks' father, and with our father and mother, who became your Baltais grandparents, I hid in the thick forest from the German soldiers."

"Then, too, Mamina?"

"Then, too. But I was so young, and it was summer. Often I was happy in the beautiful forest. It was like a great mother, sheltering me, whispering and singing to me with its soft, fragrant breath. *Jā,*" said Mamina, "there are gentle things in our world—pine forests and the sacred oaks, fields of grain and clover, rivers flowing to the sea, larks and young girls singing."

"Mamina, let Dzintra and me sing a song for you."

"Sing, my linden blossoms."

"Mother, I'll drive the cows
   To the river's bend, where the pasture is rich.
   At the bend of the river the cows eat grass.
   I sit upon the hill,
   Stitching colored mittens."

"*Jā,* that was my childhood," sighed Mamina. "Sing another song."

"We shall sing a brave song, Mamina, one of Marga's favorites."

"Then sing Marga's brave song loud and clear, that every one in the wagon train may hear and take heart."

"Sorrow, my great sorrow
   I would not heed my sorrow.
   I placed my sorrow under a stone.
   And skipped over it, singing."

Janis Bracs took up the song. Soon all the cavalcade was singing—singing its way into strange exile.

The slow wheels turned. The slow day wore on. At mid-morning a halt was made for rest and food. The animals were fed and watered. "Dear Brune, you go where we go," murmured Dzintra stroking the cow.

Before noon Tonis gave up. The girls turned sadly to see him halt in the road, trembling and whimpering, and then limp off across the fields. By noon also Brune simply laid herself down in the mud. Edvarts wheeled back from the head of the procession, urging the creature to her feet. On the road leading through the forest she lay down again. As it was almost time for more refreshments, she was allowed to rest. And while the people ate and drank and warmed their hands over a fire of brush and pine cones, a refugee couple appeared, walking. They carried two young children.

"How far have you come?" they were asked.

"By the time we reach Riga, it will be forty-five miles."

"Come into our wagon. Ride with us. Rest your burdens." Before the day was over, other footsore travelers were given aid.

The distance lessened. In mid-afternoon a wind began to blow from the sea beyond Riga. The air grew thick with fog and rain. The people huddled miserably in their shawls and blankets. Again Brune sank to her tired knees. She refused to budge. Edvarts advised Rudolfs. "Go on without us. We Darzins must wait here until Brune is somewhat rested." He told Rudolfs of the turns in the road, and the name of the back street which would admit the exiles into Riga without interference from the German guards.

No one dared to linger over the farewells, or to say,

"Shall we ever meet again?" But when *kundze* Bracs
came up, her fair round cheeks flushed, she held Mamina
close, saying, "The brave speak brave words. God keep
you, Kristine." And Janis said, "Thanks to Astra and
Dzintra, we lightened the way with song. God give us
the courage to keep singing."

The street lamps of Riga were sending glistening paths
of light on the rain-wet avenues when the weary Darzins
reached the building where Vecmamina and Uncle
Imants lived. Astra climbed the stairs to knock on their
door, and saw how Vecmamina turned pale, then red
with joy. Uncle Imants hastened down to show Edvarts
a shed which would serve as shelter for Brune and Gipsy
and the wagon, although it was a tight squeeze as to
space. Uncle insisted on feeding the animals. He persuaded the exhausted Brune to give down a scant
amount of milk. The family belongings were carried to
the apartment and the shed locked.

How good to be out of the cold and wet, and to eat a
hot supper together! Dzintra fell asleep at the table,
and was carried to bed. Astra soon laid herself down
beside her sister. Yet at first she could not rest. She
heard her father talking to Uncle Imants.

"I have been ordered to Germany to work in a factory.
Otherwise, I would have to serve as a soldier with the
Nazi forces. And as there is no longer our home in
Latvia, and we must not fall victim to the advancing
Reds, going to Germany as a laborer seems to be the
lesser evil."

"Couldn't Kristine and the girls have found safety in
Kurzeme?" asked Uncle Imants. "The German troops

still hold that Latvian province and the sea ports through which they not only draw supplies, but which may provide escape for them. Our own soldiers are helping in Kurzeme, in the hope that from there they may eventually succeed in freeing all of our land."

"Kristine did consider a Kurzeme refuge," answered Astra's father. "But how are we to know that Kurzeme will remain free? Besides, Kristine said that we should all stay together. So I asked, and the German answered, 'Your Frau may go with you if she agrees to work in the factory. How old are your Kinder?' And when I told him, he grinned and said, 'Ja, the Kinder work, too. Germany has lost many men in battle. Laborers are needed.'"

From her bed Astra cried out in dismay. "Tevs! Our little golden Dzintra will work in a factory?"

Her father came to lean over her and stroke her cheek. "We Baltic refugees do not as we wish, but as we are obliged to do," he explained gently. "This is the only way, if we are to stay together. Now say your prayers, daughter, and go to sleep."

"Will Vecmamina and Uncle Imants go with us?" whispered Astra.

"Your vecmamina says she is too old to be leaving her home land. Your uncle has decided to stay as long as he can. But he has plans for reaching safety if it becomes necessary to try."

It was a week later, in the dark, chill hours before dawn, that the four members of the Darzins family stood on the quay at Riga, waiting to board a German troop ship. They carried the few things they had been able to bring. Mamina had also made a knapsack for each, equipped with necessities—a change of underwear, soap and towel, a bit of food, a little money. "In these straps we surely look like Gipsy in his everyday harness," observed Edvarts, trying to joke. But somehow the memory of Gipsy and the fields of home caused the docks to blur and swim until the Darzins scarcely knew whether they were still ashore, or out there on the dark, trembling water.

On the heels of many others, they stumbled up the gangway to the shadowy deck. "Mamina!" cried Astra, softly, "isn't that the *kundze* Kruze ahead of us?"

"So it is, poor soul." Mamina reached out with a gentle touch.

Their old neighbor turned a tragic face. "*Jā*, I also go," she murmured. "My Elza is dead, and the Nazis drafted my young son Rolands. He is not yet sixteen. He is only a child. Perhaps in Germany I might be near him, whether or not I know it. Perhaps I might even see him. Perhaps I—" her voice trailed away in despair.

How many were on this ship, darkened in the dark harbor because of the danger of enemy bombs? It was packed with Baltic exiles and wounded German soldiers. Before they realized it, the ship moved out into the Daugava on its way to open sea. The refugees were allowed to gather on the decks for a final view of Riga's dim silhouette. In the cold rain which began to fall, and in the cold wind which blew from the sea, they sent their national hymns winging back to the land.

Suddenly a figure darted out from the group of exiles near the Darzins. Ghostlike, it fled toward the ship's rail. There was a long, sad, haunting cry, a deep splash. The ship moved inexorably on. "It was the *kundze* Kruze from Vidzeme who threw herself into the river," said one, in a tone that was low and completely final. "Ah-hhh," breathed Tevs, and his sigh became one with the sighing wind. "The poor *kundze!* After all, she could not go!"

Into the deep, stinking hold of the ship Mamina and her daughters groped their way. They laid themselves down on the straw-filled sacks in the crowded space reserved for women. Now the ship entered the heaving seas. The beams began to creak and shudder. The army horses, partitioned on the other side of the hold, stamped restlessly. Kristine Darzins reached out and laid her hands, cold but comforting, on those of her daughters, Dzintra on the one side, Astra on the other.

"Where is Tevs?" whispered Dzintra, afraid, yet daring to ask.

"He lies on the deck above us, with other Baltic fathers."

"In the rain, Mamina?" asked Astra, the tears secret on her cheeks.

"In the rain," came the answer. "But take comfort that he is here, on this ship. So many fathers have disappeared forever. Come what may," whispered Mamina, "we shall be together."

Together, thought Astra, *together except for our dear Marga, and the Baltais grandparents. Together except for Vecmamina, Uncle Imants and Eriks; the school-mates once so merry; Brune, Gipsy, Tonis, the storks.*

*Of course Mamina had not forgotten. In the dark she
hid her pain and kept back her grieving words.*

Astra resolved to stay awake until she was certain
that her mother slept. She shifted her knapsack. She
heard the restless rustle of straw sacks about her, the
trembling sighs, the stifled weeping. Now she was
indeed a true exile. At how deep a level did she and all
the exiles ride in the deep, deep sea? Swish, slap—she
heard the movement of the waters. Heave and lift, and
sink and heave—she felt the roll of the ship. When would
the slow dawn come, when—and where—the journey's
bitter end?

Like Dzintra, Astra drifted into sleep, her hand in her
mother's.

12   THE ATTIC REFUGE

Haven of God—Astra remembered the German-held port where the transport had docked after the voyage across the Baltic Sea from Riga. Among all the confusing impressions, she remembered it because its name had such a lovely sound and meaning, so lovely that for a moment her heart had lifted. But then she heard a refugee laugh in a dry, bitter way, saying, "So! We have arrived at Paradise!" He had spit over the ship's rail toward the dock, so that Astra knew the port could not, after all, be a haven offered by God. Still strapped in her knapsack harness, and with the addition of the big, tied-up bundle of family belongings on her back,

Astra clutched to her chest the can of salted sausages brought from home. Huddling close to her parents, she had stumbled down the gangplank with the other over-laden passengers. And as they were shoved into the waiting cattle trucks, Astra had felt as young and help-less as her little sister Dzintra. What was to happen to them in Germany under their German masters?

On the crowded train now taking the Darzins to the village where they had been assigned to a factory, Astra was still asking herself that question. Itching, and drowsy from lack of sleep, she thought of the past week.

The cattle trucks had delivered them to a barracks formerly used as a prison camp for captured Polish soldiers. The prisoners were gone, but the barbed wire and a few armed guards were still there. The food was surely no better than prisoners' fare—the thin, watery soup, the little piece of moldy black bread, the weak coffee, the wormy kohlrabi. Mamina had exchanged looks of horror with the two other women when they saw and smelled the room assigned to them and their fam-ilies—twelve miserable human beings. Vermin crawled on the walls. On the floor a layer of stinking straw cov-ered—what rotting pestilence? That night the three families preferred sleeping out of doors, the children in their winter coats lined with rabbit fur. The next morn-ing, while the men queued up at the barracks head-quarters to get their labor assignments, the women set to work. Armed with trench shovels, twig brooms and pails of water, it took them hours to clean the room, for at intervals they must stop, overtaken with a retching sickness. Astra, told to keep herself and Dzintra in the fresh air, had wept to think of her mother working ankle deep in the filth left by the Polish captives. But that night the families slept in the little room. It was far from spotless, but it could be endured. And by some miracle, the women had procured fresh straw to spread within the uncurtained bunks. The Darzins had lived at that dreadful camp for a week.

Yesterday, when they had boarded this train, now moving through the east German countryside, Edvarts had breathed a great sigh of relief. "Let us try to forget," he had advised, "even though the lice and bedbugs which lived in the camp have left the marks of their travels all over us." Edvarts had made such a horrible face as he pointed to the red rash on their arms and faces, it was impossible not to laugh a little if only to please him. And they were all so very glad to be going somewhere else.

Yet their glances had turned anxiously toward Dzintra, who lay in Mamina's lap, flushed with fever. "It was the bugs that carried the sickness to our little one," whispered Edvarts.

Then last night, as the train had moved slowly through blacked-out Berlin, there came the terrifying thunder of bombs. Like an animal sensing an enemy and suddenly playing dead in a dark forest path, the train shuddered to a halt. The bombs crashed. The earth trembled. The coaches rocked. Anti-aircraft guns barked. More bombs fell, more answering flak screamed upward. After a while the clamor ceased. The train crept on. "One more thing we have survived," remarked Edvarts, grimly.

This morning the tracks ran through a wide plain,

lying pale gold in the autumn sunlight. Here, hung a
shattered bridge. There, stood a ruined tower. Toward
noon two paunchy German tradesmen boarded the train
at a small station. No sooner were they seated opposite
the Darzins family, than they brought out thick sand-
wiches and flasks of wine, smacking their lips and
chewing with gusto before the eyes of their half-starved
neighbors. Presently they withdrew behind their news-
papers. After a lengthy silence, Astra whispered,
"Wouldn't I have loved to get my hands on those sand-
wiches! They were rye, spread with real butter and
thick meat." Edvarts turned a look of such deep concern
on his daughter that she began to laugh. Soon they were
all laughing a little, not from gaiety so much as em-
barrassment. A family from a Latvian farm, hungry!

The well-fed German travelers left the train at Leipzig. "I know this old city," Edvarts remarked. "More
than once I attended the great fairs here. They were
famous all over Europe. When you were a baby, Astra,
I entered some of my own craft in the exhibits, a set of
matching silver-and-amber jewelry, and an engraved
silver box. Both items won prizes, and the money I
received from their sale helped a little in buying the
home you loved in Latvia." He was silent for a moment.
"But I must confess that I do not know the region beyond Leipzig," he went on. "I am uncertain—"

Edvarts' anxiety was so apparent that the other
passengers quickly became aware of it. Here was a
poor family which must soon leave the train, but at
what station? The question was passed along until a
German traveler came to the Darzins' bench. "That

village you are bound for is not on this railway line," he said. "But at two stops from now you get off. Then you walk two miles on the road which leads to Halle. *Ja*, you walk along the country road until you come to a hill. Below, you see the village."

"There is kindness," said Mamina, when Edvarts had thanked the German. "Notice, my daughters, how in every nation live both the kind and the unkind."

"*Jā*, all the world is like that," agreed Edvarts. He rubbed his jaw in a troubled way. "But two miles of walking, carrying the sick child and our belongings!"

"We shall manage," Mamina assured him.

"And after being cramped for so long in this train, the exercise will seem good," offered Astra.

"Also, during that walk we shall have time to gather our courage for what comes next." Mamina straightened her tired shoulders.

"So!" Edvarts' glance swept over his wife and children, the coats and blankets, the boxes and bags, the suitcases. And long before the right stop came, Astra was tense on the edge of the seat, clutching the can of sausages, precious against a hungrier day than this.

What a relief to find themselves walking in the fresh air at last, even though so laden! Open fields lay on either side of the road, reminding them a little of Latvian fields. When the way led through the woods, the family rested. Dzintra opened her eyes. She saw the great, gentle boughs stirring above her; she felt the sweet silence. "Are we home again?" she asked. Astra saw how her father's answer caught in his throat, so that he could only shake his head gently.

Going on again, Astra burst out, "I wonder what the
director of the factory will be like? And his house where
we shall perhaps sleep amid the potatoes in the cellar?"

Mamina looked startled, then smiled. "In my mind I
have made a picture of the director's wife. I see her as
a stout old woman, her hair skinned back into a tight
bun, and over it a white cap. She wears a black dress,
a lace-edged apron, and at her collar an old-fashioned
brooch."

"And the director—" Astra went on, entertained by
this foolish game of guessing. "Herr Director is old and
bald and glum, and he has a stomach like this." Astra
made a large curving gesture in front of herself and her
can of sausages.

"Jā!" chuckled her father. "The German stomach is
the best fed in all Europe these days, with food seized
in conquered countries. From our Latvia, too." He
shrugged, then set his mouth firmly. "We must go to
our new master with good will, not with resentment.
Let's hope that Herr and Frau Jaffe will be kind, no
matter what they look like."

"For several years now we are used to unkindness,"
murmured Mamina. "If only we shall have a room to
ourselves, and clean beds! Ah-hh, clean beds!" sighed
Mamina. Then, in the pretty way she had lost for a
long time, she broke into laughter. "I should talk! Clean
beds for the Darzins, who are so woefully dirty! I am
ashamed to present ourselves at the Jaffe door."

"Look!" cried Astra.

Here was the hill of which they had been told. Below, in a narrow valley, lay the village. On this calm

October evening, it appeared as a cup holding peace. With mingled anxiety and hope the exiles stared at it.

Then Mamina looked about her. "See that haystack in the field by the roadside? We shall sit there while we comb our hair and make ourselves more presentable."

"If only I could shave!" complained Edvarts. "But water was never known to flow from a haystack."

Astra searched the landscape. "A stream is made to order, Tevs, below the hill." And out of Edvarts' knapsack came his razor, towel and soap. He hastened down to the stream.

"Now you look more like Edvarts Darzins and less like a bearded lion," Mamina complimented him, when he returned freshly shaven. With his wet towel she wiped her face and those of her daughters. Dzintra got weakly to her feet. The fresh air, and the water on her cheeks made her feel better. And now, their braids neat, the girls followed their parents down the hill and into the village.

The shops were shuttered and the streets quite deserted, for it was the supper hour. Directions were asked of two boys playing ball. Afterward Astra heard the younger one asking his playmate, "Those skinny ones are not of the Fatherland?"

"*Na,*" came the answer. "They are no doubt Polish prisoners come with bag and baggage to work in the Jaffe factory."

Astra burned to flounce around and cry out, "We are Latvians, of Latvia!"

A high wooden fence surrounded the Jaffe property. The barbed wire strung along its top appeared hostile.

But the big gate stood open. "I had better go to the door, while you wait." Edvarts decided. Almost at once he returned. His eyes were bright. "The director says the gate was left open this evening because we were expected." Edvarts ventured a hurried whisper. "It's a fine large house Herr Jaffe has."

Astra's heart set up such a thumping that surely the can of sausages would begin banging against her chest. Once through the gate, she caught glimpses of ample lawns studded with shrubbery and flower beds. But it was the house, and the people who lived in the house, that meant so terribly much to nervous strangers. Astra studied Herr Jaffe, who waited in the doorway.

"He doesn't just beam with welcome," Astra told herself. "But he is almost smiling. And except for the round, well-fed stomach, he doesn't look at all as I pictured him. He is no older than my father."

Within the entrance hall, Herr Jaffe turned and called, "The workers from Riga have arrived." Whereupon his wife promptly appeared. She was also of a sleek roundness. But she had a lovely pink-and-white skin. Her fair braids were wound into a shining coronet. She was dressed stylishly, as if for an afternoon party, and in truth, she had been attending one. *Ah, but my own Mamina would be far prettier than Frau Jaffe, if she were dressed so beautifully, and after a month, perhaps, of good eating!*

"I had thought that both daughters were of an age to work in the factory," observed the director, staring critically at Dzintra.

Edvarts smiled, although uneasily. "You will find that the quality of my work will make up for the lack of a fourth pair of hands," he declared. And Mamina added, rather out of place, "Our least one is still ailing from the life we have been obliged to lead since fleeing from our homeland."

Herr Jaffe made a gesture of impatience. But his wife leaned over and lifted Dzintra up in her arms. "The poor Kinder should be in bed," she crooned. "Come now, above."

Astra could not resist a secret jubilant squeeze of Mamina's hand as they followed the strong-stepping matron up two flights of stairs. *The German Hausfrau so kind to little Dzintra! The fluttering hope for comfortable quarters within this house!*

The attic room was spotless. Two double beds were dressed out in white, and the fat, feather-filled *plumeaux* common in German bedrooms were snowily encased. There was a table, a huge standing wardrobe, a washstand, one straight chair and a rocker. The dormer windows stood open to the pale evening sky. The air flowing in had a mild, autumnal freshness.

"Your home!" said the Frau, placing Dzintra in the rocker. "And now—" This unfinished sentence had something to do with her hasty departure. She could be heard tripping down the stair.

Presently, in answer to a faint knock, Astra opened the door to a charming surprise. In trotted three little girls, carrying cups and spoons with an important air of ceremony. They were plump and pink-cheeked like their parents. The tallest said she was eight years old. "We are Bertha, Blanka, and Betta. And comes the Mutter with something for you."

It was a big kettle of soup which Frau Jaffe brought, steaming and fragrant, with fresh black bread to crumb in it. "My husband says that when you have eaten and your children are in bed, you must come downstairs. He wants to show you the factory yet tonight, for in the morning you go early to work, and no time to waste."

Edvarts nodded in agreement. "*Jā,* we must see the factory."

And Mamina said, her eyes lustrous, "Please, Frau Director, we thank you for the soup, and for the clean white beds. You cannot know—" Mamina had not the words to express her gratitude for simple cleanliness. "But we are so dirty. Please, might we have water for bathing?"

After the soup and bread Edvarts and Kristine went below, returning with a tin tub, cans of hot water, and clean shirts loaned as sleeping garments. After her bath, Dzintra murmured drowsily from her bed, "Tevs, I am not sick any more. I am well."

"Cleanliness is health," answered her father. "*Jā,* now I can kiss my Janiti without getting my dirty face dirtier." Dzintra fell asleep with her fever gone and laughter on her lips.

When all were bathed and her parents had gone with Herr Jaffe, Astra lay so relaxed she felt as if she were drifting feather-light in space. A long time later, or so it seemed, she floated up out of a deep sleep. In the darkness she heard her father say, "In the factory,

Kristine, I could tell that Herr Jaffe was very pleased to discover that I am as good a craftsman as he is. *Jā!*" exclaimed Edvarts, and Astra knew he had the right to speak well of himself—"a *master* craftsman!"

"Certainly that," Mamina agreed. "And though we are to be paid slave wages, and I doubt if we shall be able to fatten our children to the plumpness of Bertha, Blanka and Betta—"

"At least we shall earn enough to keep our souls and bodies together," Edvarts finished.

"It is too early to say," ventured Mamina, cautiously, "but I think it may not be so bad here. Perhaps, as exiles, we are lucky."

Astra called out softly. "We are clean, Mamina. We have a room to ourselves."

"Do you talk in your sleep, eavesdropper?" asked her father.

"Tevs, what is the factory like?"

"You will see. But I have told you that it manufactures the metal parts for German army uniforms, such as buttons, belt buckles, and insignia, as well as army stamps and seals."

Astra lay still, thinking how insane it seemed, considering centuries of history, that a Latvian should work for the German Army. *Nē*, nothing made sense any more! "Tevs," she called, "what work am I to do in the factory?"

"I do not know yet," answered her father. "We live from day to day. Now say a prayer. Then sleep well between the clean sheets."

"I will tell you, though," said Mamina from across the

attic room. "Tomorrow I am to be allowed to stay away
from the factory, so that I may wash our soiled clothes.
At the same time, I am to do the Jaffe's household
laundry. It is to be a regular arrangement."

"*Nē*, Mamina!" cried Astra.

"Hush! Never mind! Beggars cannot be choosers.
You are fourteen. You will help me. In German house-
holds the laundry is done only about every two months,
and in winter but once, perhaps. In spring comes a week
or more of the soap, the hot water, the hot iron, until
everything is clean. So a family must have many linens
and clothes to last the winter through. This evening
Frau Jaffe told me this, and she showed me her store
of linens, snowy stack upon stack, each dozen tied with
yellow ribbons. *Jā*, my eyes bugged like a frog's, staring
at the Hausfrau's wealth." Mamina's voice suddenly
warmed. "I have been promised a reward when we
finish the laundry."

Lavish possibilities formed airily in Astra's mind. It
was something to look forward to—that un-named reward!

"Mamina, shall we not soon have word from Vecmamina, answering the letter you wrote from the camp,
giving her the Jaffe address?"

"We hope for an answer."

"*Hope*. Mamina, I never knew it was a word that
meant so much."

"You are young to have learned what it truly means,"
answered Mamina. "Hope is the first breath of morning.
It is the day's bread. It is the prayer at night."

13

PILING UP GOLD

It was early evening. Astra, Dzintra, and Mamina were in the attic room. They were laughing so hard that Astra had collapsed on one of the beds. Dzintra was writhing on the floor. At first she had not been certain it was a thing to laugh about. But to share such side-splitting mirth with Mamina and Astra—what a long time had passed since they had done it! Moreover, a wonderful spice was added because they must stifle their laughter. Frau Jaffe must not hear. Dzintra, cramming her braids into her mouth, looked at Mamina, and was seized with another attack of giggles. Oh, Mamina, sitting in the rocker, gazing down at the small object in her lap! One minute she would screw her face into the most crest-fallen lines. The next minute she would pretend to be dazzled, then absolutely haughty with pride. Finally she would be overcome by her own comic play-acting, and fairly choke with suppressed laughter.

"What on earth goes on here?" Edvarts asked. They had not heard him coming up the stair. He was still wearing his factory apron. His sleeves were rolled up. His hands were dirty. Although he was plainly puzzled, he, too, began to laugh. It was contagious.

Mamina managed to pull her face into seriousness. With her hand she hid the object in her lap. Placidly she began to rock back and forth, while the girls watched in delight. "Edvarts," began Mamina, "for two days Astra and I have washed. We washed our own clothes, dirty since we docked at that—haven of God. We have washed the shirts and panties, the nightgowns and nightcaps of Bertha, Blanka, and Betta. We have washed their little dresses and pinafores. We have washed the clothing, under and outer, of Herr Director and his lady. The factory aprons we washed, and the mansion's table and bed linens. Everything we washed. We filled and emptied tubs. We soaped. We scrubbed. We squeezed. We hung out. For two more days we ironed. Edvarts, our few clothes and the Jaffe's many are snowy clean. They are polished with the hot iron to a dazzling gloss. Edvarts, for our four days' toil Madam Jaffe gave us a reward. I now show you!" Dramatically, Mamina held forth her palm. On it lay—an egg!

Edvart Darzins stared, while the girls waited mirthfully for the roars he would be obliged to choke down.

But he said nothing. He did not even smile. He was gazing at Mamina with a deep, tender compassion, and
suddenly she covered her face with her hands. She was
sobbing, and Tevs and Astra were quick to comfort her.
Dzintra stood off, trembling with dismay. Within the
span of her seven years, she had never seen her mother
cry.

But Mamina now stood up, brushing her eyes with
quick impatience. She managed a shaky laugh. "Forget
these silly tears," she cried. "Forget them, my little
one." She leaned over Dzintra, caressing her. "It was
only that I was tired," she explained to all. "It was only
that my tears of merriment somehow turned into real
tears." Mamina walked to the table, placing the egg in a
cup. "The reward—it is still absurd," she said. "But in
all fairness to Frau Jaffe, eggs are very scarce in Germany."

"I will find eggs," promised Edvarts, recklessly. "I will
bring you eggs if I have to squeeze the hens and rob the
nests. Now, Kristine, you are to rest yourself from toiling
so hard. Astra, the supper!" He marched Mamina back
to the rocking chair.

"Supper cooks in the kettle," Astra assured him. She
and Dzintra flew about, cheerfully. But there were whispers, and when Mamina sat down, the egg lay in a saucer
at her plate, coddled to perfection, and the family circle
of faces bright with a Christmas-gift kind of radiance.

Mamina would have it no other way than that everyone should dip a spoonful from the saucer. "This little
egg may give each of us a Jaffe fatness!" she cried, gaily.
Who would have thought, back in Latvia where they had

their own hens, that an egg could be so rare and precious! "But, *jā*, we knew it even in Latvia," Astra recalled, "after the Communists took over."

The three-story factory building stood near the Jaffe house, behind the same high fence. The next morning Mamina took her place among its fifty workers. By evening her muscles were so sore she could not move without groaning. "I plane the metal plates smooth for the engraving," she explained to her daughters, "and my arms go back and forth hour after hour. But I shall get used to it," she assured them cheerfully. "And I shall do my work well. For if I do not, Herr Director will slap my cheek."

"Mamina, are you joking? The director slaps?" gasped Astra.

"If he must tell the worker a second time what is not first understood, the director slaps. He slaps if the worker fails to keep up a certain pace. Today I saw the cheek of a young woman redden under the flat of his palm. And he struck the old watchmaker who did business across the street from your father's shop in Riga." Mamina related all this calmly.

"Herr Jaffe does not mean to be harsh, I think," Edvarts interrupted. "It is his way. Last evening I saw him slap his little Blanka when she did not instantly obey. But—" Edvarts' eyes flashed, "Herr Director will not slap my wife."

"If for no other reason, husband, he respects you above all other workers because your skill is as great as his own," Mamina said. "Besides," she continued, her eyes twinkling, "when he slapped today he noticed the little mystifying look I gave him. It was perhaps like the small smile of the Mona Lisa, and I think it made him wonder."

Edvarts laughed. "My Kristine, you can't expect to alter a factory manager's habits with a Mona Lisa smile." He changed the subject. "Today I spoke to our boss about school for our children."

"And what did he say?" demanded Astra, eagerly. Dzintra echoed her.

Their father laid a comforting hand on Astra. "Herr Director said that Dzintra is useless for work. Therefore she may attend the village day school with Bertha and Blanka. But he said, 'Your Astra will have no time for school. *Ja*, already she helps *meine Frau* with the sweeping and dusting. She will shine the windows and clean the bricks at the doorstep. She will keep bright the cage of the canaries. She will carry slops to the pigs. She will be "mamsell" to our little Betta, and do the braids of our Bertha and Blanka. You understand, Darzins, my wife is an excellent Hausfrau, but she is fond of society. She must have time to mingle with the women of her own rank, and to attend her Frauenklub. She likes to take a bus to Halle or to Leipzig sometimes, for shopping or the cinema.'

"So that's that, my Astra." Her father's eyes were so sad that she pretended not to care.

"Tevs, what fine German housewifery I shall learn!" she exclaimed.

"Some day you may catch up with school," sighed Mamina. "Daughter, will it be good news when I tell you that the young woman I saw slapped today is—well —some one you admired in Latvia?"

Astra felt breathless. "It couldn't be," she faltered. "*Nē*, I am ashamed to hope. Mamina, is it—*jaunkundze* Zaiga Kimenis?"

"The very same!"

"And I failed to recognize her?" Edvarts asked, regretfully.

"Zaiga is so thin and changed," Mamina explained. "But how she brightened when we looked across the loft at one another, and looked again, and then were sure! I am thinking," mused Mamina, "perhaps it could be arranged for Zaiga Kimenis to give lessons to Astra."

"Oh-hh!" breathed Astra. "If only the *jaunkundze* may teach me again, what do I care being slavey to Frau Jaffe? You know, if I were going to high school in Latvia as it used to be, I would be studying English this year. Now, in Germany, might I not learn it from Zaiga Kimenis?"

"Does she know English?" inquired Tevs.

"Of course!" cried Astra. "She is a graduate of the University of Riga. And once she visited the British Isles, and all summer would allow herself to speak nothing but English."

"We have no money to pay a teacher."

How well Astra knew it! Her lips quivered. But suddenly her eyes became starry. "Tevs, the sausages!" she caroled. "We could pay Zaiga with sausages!"

"*Jā!*" agreed Mamina, with delight. "The sausages we carried into exile for a time of hunger! And now a hunger for learning burns in our Astra."

But Dzintra, who was simply hungry in her stomach,

ran her tongue over her lips greedily. "Shall we have a
supper party with the sausages?"

"Bless the ravenous child!" Mamina sang out. "*Jā*, a
party to bring light to poor Zaiga Kimenis, and to us all!
We do not forget how to laugh and sing a little. And
there will be the platter on the table, holding a sausage
for Dzintra, a sausage for Astra, one for Zaiga, one for
Tevs, one for Kristine."

"And then, after the party," Astra went on, "Tevs will
ask it. '*Jaunkundze* Zaiga,' Tevs will begin, 'could you
find time and strength to teach English to Astra? For
pay we have only sausages, of which there are many left
in the can.' "

The evening of the party arrived. At first, when Zaiga
Kimenis put her arms around Astra, neither of them
could speak for joy. Then, around the table, family and
guest chattered together. The sausages were wonderful.
Zaiga had brought a cherished jar of Latvian honey.
Tevs had walked two miles into the country and bought
potatoes and apples without having to sacrifice any
precious ration allowance. "I have an apple tree at
home," Dzintra proudly informed Zaiga.

"And the honey reminds me," began Astra. With
thoughts of Marga, who had loved the words which
spangled her native folkways, Astra sang:

> "Nothing can surpass the honor
>   of the bee.
> In the fog she piles up gold.
> Sitting in the sun
> She prepares a golden crown."

But for everyone the evening was made important with talk of the English lessons.

"What joy to teach my young friend Astra again!" agreed Zaiga. "But *nē*, I will not take your sausages. As soon as possible I shall go into Leipzig for an English grammar and dictionary."

"Of course I will pay your bus fare, and for the grammar-dictionary," beamed Edvarts. "Ah-hh, in learning English, shall not our Astra 'pile up gold,' like the bee?"

Plaiting three sets of young Jaffe braids and those of her sister, scrubbing the doorstep bricks or the kitchen tiles, carrying slops, Astra rehearsed her English. Her hands grew rough and her knees scarred. She was thin as a sapling. She was a young slavey, but her mind was free and soaring. On Saturday nights or Sunday afternoons she recited to *jaunkundze* Kimenis.

A long-delayed letter arrived. "It is from brother Imants," announced Edvarts, excitedly. "Imants does not sign his name, but I know."

For your message Zenta—that was Vecmamina—*sends thanks. Tell the girls that the good cow Brune saved several little ones from starvation. Riga fell to the Soviets on October the thirteenth. A curtain has descended. I will manage to send this from another place. Writing or receiving letters is dangerous. All of life is dangerous. Love from us both, and God keep you.*

The snows of winter covered the earth. Christmas was spare, although a little festive with greens from the woods. The Jaffe's sent a gift of Apfelwein, also a piece of pork from one of their freshly butchered hogs. January seemed to drag endlessly. Then one Saturday evening, Zaiga Kimenis presented Astra with a package.

"Open it! Please open it!" begged Dzintra, while the others gathered around eagerly.

Trembling a little, Astra untied the string and drew off the paper. "Oh!" she whispered. In her hands lay a book, and under her finger tips the exciting *feel* of a book. With delight she read aloud the English words on the cover, "*The Secret Garden*—what a beautiful title!" Rapidly she riffled the pages. "The text is in English."

Zaiga nodded, smiling. "The Leipzig bookseller informed me that this is a story much loved by girls and boys of England and America," she said.

Then Astra discovered what the *jaunkundze* had written on the flyleaf, in English. "For my dear pupil, Astra Darzins, in reward for good work done. Zaiga Kimenis. January, 1945."

Astra found herself blinking away tears, and in her happiness, jumping up to embrace first her teacher, then each member of her family.

"Now read to us something from the book," demanded Dzintra. And when Astra obliged, rather haltingly, and with help from Zaiga, Tevs shook his head in bewilderment. "The English speech is outlandish," he muttered. "I know Russian. I know German. But never shall I learn English, never! But my Astra learns!" He was proud.

The Darzins and Zaiga Kimenis had need to store up the happiness of such an hour. For now came the fearful days and nights when the big allied bombers roared over

the village to drop their shells and phosphor flares
into cities. How lightly one learned to sleep, nerves taut
and muscles twitching! At those ear-splitting sounds one
became a creature of pell-mell flight, a creature of hiding. Down the stairs, down, down into the deep darkness
of the cellar, where many a night both families spread
their blankets or feather covers on the mounds of Jaffe
potatoes. They would lie listening. Would the bombs
crash through the house this time? Would the walls
come tumbling upon them, and their bodies be of little
more consequence than the potatoes?

As January passed and February merged into March,
Herr Jaffe became quite thin. Fretfully he declared that
the bombers were becoming more frequent. And such
ridiculous war news! The Darzins often heard him
shouting his angry unbelief. "What if our ally Italy did
surrender months ago? Alone we are strong. *Ja*, I
know that our Wehrmacht had to quit in France. Something went wrong there. But this outlandish rumor that
the Russians may advance on Berlin!" Herr Jaffe snorted.
"Why, Berlin is Europe's largest city! In Berlin no enemy has set foot for a century and half. *Ja*, they say that
other allied forces have fought their way past our western borders, and—" Herr Jaffe's voice dropped to a super-
stitious whisper. "Some say that the enemy is determined
to cross the Rhine. *Ach*, our beloved and lovely river—
they will not dare—they can never cross! There are many
strong bridges. Besides, do we not have our wonder
weapons?"

Early in March the American First Army crossed the
Rhine. In the weeks that followed, the allies took town

after town, city after city, in their sweep eastward. By
April bombs were falling all over Germany. The Americans were drawing a siege arc around Leipzig. The arc
took in the village where Herr Jaffe's house stood as the
largest and finest, and his factory as the most important
industry.

Preceded by an exhausting night of bombing, hel-
meted doughboys entered the village. Their guns
trained, they crept warily around corners, watching for
snipers. It was not long before total surrender hung
from windows in the shape of sheets, pillow slips, and
even feather beds.

So the occupation forces took over the Jaffe house.
Madam wept aloud when the officers moved into her
large, handsome rooms, leaving but one bedroom and the
kitchen for her and her family. "We stay here only until
Berlin is captured and Hitler surrenders," the officer assured her. He closed the factory, drily remarking, "The
German Army has no present need of uniform insignia."

When the soldiers explored the house and entered
the Darzins' attic room, there were a few moments of
panic. "Where is your uniform?" asked the officer of
Edvarts.

"The American thinks you are a German soldier,"
whispered Mamina. "We must make him understand, or
it means prison for you."

"Latvian! I am Latvian!" protested Edvarts to the
officer.

Apparently the American had never heard of Latvia.
Mamina seized one of Dzintra's crayons. On the floor
she tried to draw a map. But she was not a draughtsman.

Her hand shook. The outlines of the Baltic shores were far from true.

Astra had been standing dumbly by until she realized that her mother was getting nowhere with the American officer, and that her father seemed paralyzed. If only she could think of the right words, she might explain. But her mind was a blank. Hastily she snatched up her English-Latvian dictionary, and scanning it, found the key word she needed. "Refugees!" she cried. "Are refugees from Baltic!" She pointed to Mamina's crooked map. "October, nineteen hundred forty-four, we—we run from Communists. Please, we are not Germans. Please, our country has German enemy thousand years."

The officer smiled. "I understand," he said. "You mean that the German nation has been your traditional enemy for thousands of years."

That evening, when rations were sent in for the staff officers, the Darzins were generously included. Such food as they had not dreamed of for months—big, fat meat balls, mashed potatoes, cabbage, fruit cocktail, real coffee. "We gobble!" laughed Mamina. "Our hungry stomachs, shrunken to smallness—can they hold all this?"

"Jā, Mamina, they hold!" cried Dzintra, blissfully stuffing herself.

The youngest American officer in the Jaffe house was called Bill. Astra showed him her English copy of The Secret Garden. "Gosh!" Bill exclaimed, grinning. "I'd almost forgotten that book. When I was a kid in Kalamazoo our school put on a dramatization of it. I played

the part of—now, wait a minute—wasn't his name Dick-
on?"

Mamina did some mending for the Americans. At
their urgent request she fried a mountain of potato chips,
and asked for the lard they would have thrown away
afterward in the wasteful American manner. Now and
then wonderful gifts were left in the attic room, canned
food, coffee, fresh eggs which had surely been conjured
up through some mysterious Yankee sorcery; cigarettes
which could be traded for almost anything. The Jaffes
received coffee also, but no food. The fair and innocent
three, Bertha, Blanka and Betta were made happy with
chocolate bars. Dzintra's mouth was often an ecstatic
chocolate smear. "I think," said Astra to the youngsters,
"that Kalamazoo in America must be paved solidly with
chocolate."

With the closing of the factory, Edvarts found work
among Polish exiles at a large market garden outside the
village. It was spring, and time to transplant from green-
house to garden.

But about the first of May, when Berlin surrendered
and Hitler's suicide was announced, Edvarts began hearing alarming rumors. "I must find out for sure," he said.
He took the bus into Leipzig to talk with Latvian refugees he knew there. When he returned he was nervous
and excited.

"Tomorrow we leave the Jaffe house," he announced.
"I have managed to find a car and driver. He promises
to pick us up at five o'clock in the morning, also the
watchmaker and his wife, and Zaiga Kimenis. At Leip-

zig we catch the last train out before the Russians take over the city and all this eastern zone. *Jā,* we'll catch that train before the Communists catch us."

None but Dzintra slept that night. What if the driver failed to bring the car? What if the arrival at Leipzig were too late? What if that last train had departed?

"Tevs, where are we going this time?" asked Dzintra the next morning.

"To the west," he answered. "Somewhere in the American zone."

Somewhere!

14   A LOAD OF FREIGHT

Slowly the long string of box cars jolted through the German countryside. Men sprawled on the roofs, clinging like cats. Inside, the people were packed to the last inch of space. Some were obliged to stand. Seated on the dirty floor, others rocked upon their suitcases, bundles, coats and blankets. In their laps lay more belongings—packets of food, cans, baskets, bags, boxes, and here and there something valuable, a camera, a fine leather portfolio, a kit of prized tools, a loved book. At each lurch of the train the refugees swayed and pitched. Remembering the space and dignity of the homes where they had once dwelt in cherished privacy, they looked at one another in shame for themselves, and in shame for a world in which such a plight could befall honorable men and women. Was freedom worth all this misery and humiliation? "*Jā, jā!* How dearly we have learned that personal freedom is the most precious of all human possessions! To regain it, how far we have fled! For its sake we flee again—how far? We suffer, perhaps we die for freedom's sake."

Aboard the freight were not only Baltic refugees, but people from White Russia and the Ukraine, from Poland and East Germany. From all over the eastern zone they had rushed to catch this train, the last to leave Leipzig under American direction. A day later, an hour later, the Communists would be taking over. To escape them— that was the critical necessity.

Yesterday, in the Jaffe house, the Frau had tried to argue with Mamina. "I have heard how people like you Darzins fall dead by the wayside in their exhausting effort to escape the Russians. Little love I have for them myself, yet I have heard how the Russians and Americans have the same kind of home government. So what is the difference?"

Mamina had cried out against such ignorance. "Madam, you do not know what you say! In Latvia our president told us about America. Our books told us. In America the soul and body of each person is free. We know there is a great difference, for we have lived and died under the Russians. They trampled our flag and put up their own. They shouted in our ears, 'This Communism we give you—it is the best political system. Follow it, or die at our hands!' They took away my beautiful young daughter, my mother and my father. My neighbors—where are they? My country? I have none, except in my heart! If we die by the wayside, we die free."

When Mamina stopped because she was too shaken to go on, Astra began. "I will say it, too, Madam. Under the Nazi tyranny it was not as brutal as under the Soviets, but it was bad enough."

"I do not listen to the Fräulein's impertinence," fumed Frau Jaffe. "Before you came I had scarcely heard of Latvia, a tiny country of no importance. Let me tell you! We Germans suffer also, for our ruined cities and our dead. You are frantic to reach the American zone in the west. Didn't you know that the soldiers you thought so kind and generous plundered my house?"

The Darzins had not seen any plundering, and they knew that Frau Jaffe expressed her bitterness in many false accusations. Yet they could imagine that the Yanks, so young and light of heart, so elated with victory, had perhaps broken official rules and helped themselves to a few of the Frau's linens for a beloved "mom" in Kalamazoo or Mauch Chunk.

But this morning, when good-byes were said, Mamina had whispered, "God keep you safe, Frau Jaffe, and your family. Wars are indeed cruel to us all, whatever nation we call our own."

The Jaffes had answered with kindness. The Frau had given Mamina a can of blood pudding, rich in vitamins. Herr Jaffe had handed Edvarts a one-hundred-mark note. The pink cheeks of Bertha, Blanka, and Betta had glistened with tears as they gazed their last at Dzintra. Into Astra's hand they had thrust a paper bag of ripe cherries.

It was cherry season. The big doors of the box cars stood partly open to the summer air as Astra spoke to the watchmaker's wife. "Oldmother, do you know that this is June the twenty-fourth, and the festival of St. John?"

For a moment the oldmother's face brightened, then fell into lines of deeper sorrow. "If we could have kept the peaceful days at home," she answered, "the green boughs would be up. There would be the weaving and wearing of the wreaths. On the hills where beacon fires tell all the land that it is Ligo-Janis Day, there would be singing and dancing."

When the train halted to allow the travelers to walk about in a summer grove, they gathered green branches because in Latvia they would on this day have done the same. Crowded into the cars again, they held the leaves against their cheeks, sniffing their cool fragrance. Falteringly, Zaiga Kimenis ventured to sing:

"What should we wish
 St. John's mother today?
 Long life, good luck
 And health from heaven."

But health, good luck, and even the prospect of long life seemed so unlikely to these haggard pilgrims that the song died away amid tears.

After the halt at the wood, Dzintra noticed a young man standing near her. He was holding a fretful baby. Braced between his feet was a bundle. A violin case was strapped on his back. He appeared so worn and distressed that Dzintra lifted her arms. "Might I hold the baby for you?" she offered.

Gratefully the young man lowered the child into Dzintra's lap. He answered Mamina's glance, roving in search of the baby's mother. "*Nē, kundze,* my wife is not here. The week the bombs fell on the German spinning factory where we worked, we were showered with bricks and dust. *Kundze,* it was a very long week in the cellar full of our choking and coughing, full of our fear and hunger. It took the life of my wife, and left me with our baby son."

"What is Baby's name?" asked Dzintra. "How old is he?"

"*Janis* is his name. He is six months old."

"A true St. John's Day child, poor mite!" crooned Mamina, her pitying hand light on the baby. He was cruelly scrawny. Under the thin skin at his temples the veins showed enlarged and blue.

"Janiti is hungry all the time," mourned the father.

Dzintra felt a surge of small-mother tenderness. "Janiti!" The pet name was like an echo of her own father's love for her. How often he had called her that, because she was to have been a boy!

But something more than echo was now heard. It was music from the young father's violin. The travelers listened, soothed and dreaming, to beloved old Latvian

songs and the music of masters. "Remember?" whispered
Mamina, her eyes lustrous in the half-light. "We used
to hear that at the opera house in Riga."

When the violinist had finished the selection, he said,
"I played in the orchestra there."

It was wonderful, then, what pride and affection the
Latvian exiles felt for this skilled performer. A moment
before he had been but another forlorn wanderer, sharing their lot. But now they honored him, begging for
more music. Astra persuaded him to take her place on
the family suitcase, so that he would not become tired.

An hour later, when the freight stopped, it was along
the country roadsides and the edges of open meadows
that the travelers rambled and rested. Amid a clump of
trees a half-mile away stood a farmhouse. "I shall try to
buy milk for my Janiti there, if you will hold him for me
a little longer," said the musician. Dzintra, proud of her
responsibility, saw him hurry across the field, his violin
on his back, and disappear into the copse.

The halt seemed more brief than usual when the "all-
aboard" command was heard. The travelers scrambled
into the cars. There was a lurch forward. Gathering
speed, the train trundled swiftly ahead.

"The baby's father!" cried Dzintra, after a hasty scanning of faces. Through the open doors, the people craned
to catch a glimpse of the farmhouse, now growing
smaller in the distance. "There he is!" cried Astra. The
young man was leaping across the fields toward the
tracks. His mouth was open, as he shouted in vain.
With the baby's filled bottle in upraised hand, he made
frantic signals. The train swept around a curve. The

wood, the farmhouse, the frenzied father were lost to
view.

"One more thing to rend the heart!" cried the watchmaker's wife, brokenly. "Can't we notify the engineer?"
cried another. "*Nē*, we cannot. This is not a passenger
train, with corridors leading through. There are many
box cars between us and the engineer." . . . "Can the
musician catch up with us?" . . . "Impossible, unless he
had wings." . . . "But surely he will find us sooner or
later, and his baby." . . . "Ah, but the tracks twist and
turn, and we ourselves know not where we go. Into the
American zone, *jā*, but there are many camps there,
crowded with countless refugees like us." . . . "What was
the musician's name?" . . . "Alack, it is bad—we do not
know his name."

"Oh, Mamina, what will become of this little Janis,
without a mother, and now without a father?"

"God knows," answered Mamina sadly.

"But he was left with me." How tightly that tiny hand
clutched Dzintra's forefinger! "Mamina, in August I
shall be eight."

"Eight years old, or eighty?" A tear suddenly slid
down Mamina's cheek. *Why the tear?* thought Dzintra,
trying to imagine herself eighty years old. She laughed.
"If I were eighty, Mamina, then I would be the baby's
oldmother."

"Little oldmother!" echoed Mamina, lifting and holding, as precious gold, one of Dzintra's braids. "*Jā*, child,
until something can be done with the baby, or until his
father finds him, we shall somehow have to care for
him."

"Somehow—" At the next halt Edvarts succeeded in buying milk for Janiti.

All through the night, all through the following day and the next, the train carried its load of human freight. And as darkness of the third night fell, a fear which had been small at Leipzig and had traveled small but nagging through the miles, grew into monstrous size and shape.

The watchmaker announced, "By my compass I see that this train goes east and north as often as it goes west and south."

"Jā, why does the train loop and turn, back and switch, through a land we do not know?"

"But there are many bombed-out bridges. On account of them, perhaps the engineer must switch to other tracks before he can reach the main line."

"Oh, that engineer! For an hour past we have been traveling east. Jā, jā, we have been betrayed! Even though the Americans did provide this train, the Russians have managed to bribe the engineer! He is taking us back into the Soviet zone!"

The men huddled over a tattered map, trying to find the names of the railroad stations which flashed past in the murk. It was a night of sickening fear.

But the next day the stations of southwest Germany were hailed with trembling relief. From the spires and towers of towns fluttered the American flag. "It is the American zone at last!"

That afternoon, in the country outside Göppingen, the freight was flagged down by American military police. A fleet of army trucks was soon trundling the weary refugees to camp. It was a huge one, formerly used by the German air force. The barracks now served as living quarters for displaced persons. But time had been short. None of the allied zones was ready for the hordes of refugees sweeping down upon it.

"First come, first served here," Edvarts Darzins remarked, grimly overlooking the bewildered, milling crowds. "I think we shall have to bed down tonight where we can, and in the manner of packed sardines."

"We must find out if there is milk to be had for the small Janiti," said Mamina, rocking the wailing baby in her arms.

"*Jā, kundze,* and for my little granddaughter." A Latvian woman standing nearby held a pale child. "I wonder where—"

There was a sudden stir among the people. Sharp uneasiness seemed to jump from elbow to elbow. Whispers leaped from lip to lip. "See those Red Army officers? What are they doing here? Are we never to escape the Reds? What are they saying?"

Excited murmurs spread the truth among the exiles. "We come to the Americans, seeking refuge from the Russians. Yet Russian officers are allowed in this camp. The Soviet flag flies high. To be allowed—it is a part of senseless war dickering. But beware! As usual, the Reds are up to no good. With sweet talk they will try to lure us back to our homelands and slavery. Stuff your ears, countrymen. It is dangerous to listen."

However, the grandmother murmured into Mamina's

ear. "Ah, but did you hear what those Red officers say? They have food for our children. They have plenty of fresh, sweet milk. They invite us to come after it."

Mamina thrust Janis into Zaiga's arms. She took the baby girl from her grandmother and handed her to Astra. "Let us go quickly," she urged the grandmother. "For the sake of these little ones we shall accept from the Communists, and lose nothing but our pride."

"Watch yourselves. Be on your guard," warned Edvarts.

It was some time before the women returned. Mamina was laughing a little, although without mirth. She related what had happened.

"The Latvian grandmother told me that she is the *kundze* Zilava, from near Rezekne. She is a strong soul, that *kundze*. She handled the affair of the milk. I did not need to lift my voice.

"Well, inside the Russian building we were bowed into the cellar like a pair of ballerinas. Once there, how our eyes popped! How our mouths watered! Such stores of tempting food, great wheels of cheese, real coffee, fresh meat, cans of milk! We could have anything we chose. All it took in exchange was the filling out of questionnaires, and our signatures at the end. Where had we lived in Latvia? What work did we do? Had we left relatives there? What are their names? Why did we leave our dear homeland? Would we like to go back? *Nē? Jā?* So you see how we were expected to write down the history of our lives.

"We stared at those papers. We stared at each other. And we backed away from that pen as from a bomb with a burning fuse. *Kundze* Zilava's face went red. It went white. She cried out to the food-keepers, 'Communists! Let the good sweet milk clabber in the cans! Let our babies die better!' Then we walked out, trembling. Oh, it is folly to go near the Reds and their tricks!"

That night a summer rain fell upon the air field and upon many refugees huddling wretchedly in their coats. The rain sent a faint freshness into the barracks where Astra and Dzintra lay with Mamina, Zaiga, and baby Janis. They had taken possession of the narrow space under a long center table. The floor under their bodies was bare. They were unwashed and miserable. Yet the shelter of the table top gave them a meager sense of privacy from the mob around them. To Dzintra, especially, the table meant security for the delicate sleeping body of the baby. Amid the sighs and snores and smells, Dzintra's hand stole out to touch him.

"Janiti," whispered the little girl, "if I could, I would sing you a funny song I know about Gailiti the rooster. . . . But *nē*, it might not seem funny in such a strange place as this, or to these sad strangers around us. But tomorrow, or surely the next day, I will sing it for you. . . . Janiti, until your father finds you, I shall be your little oldmother. It was *so* nice when Mamina called me that!"

15   IN THE CAMPS

Little oldmother—in August of 1945, when Dzintra lay ill in a children's hospital fifteen miles from that first displaced persons' camp, she fretted about baby Janis. Whether she was herself, or out of her head with fever, she was forever asking, "Is he still with us, Mamina? . . . Tevs, has the baby's father taken him away?" Sometimes her dry lips mumbled words about Grandmother Baltais' lost *sakta*. In her delirium her desire for it merged with the story of *The Secret Garden*, which she had heard from Astra. "Tell me, bird in the garden, where Grandmother hid her *sakta!*" she would plead.

Almost every day Kristine or Edvarts traveled those

weary miles to see Dzintra in the hospital. Sometimes they walked, or hitched a ride by army truck. A Polish exile in the camp sometimes lent his bicycle. It was whispered that the Pole had stolen the bicycle from a German of the region. Mamina didn't care, just so the trip to the hospital was accomplished. In her worry, Mamina grew very thin. Some of the child patients did not get well. Twice Mamina had been asked to carry heartbreaking messages to parents in the Göppingen camp.

And then arose the matter of Dzintra's braids. That day when the doctor had pronounced Dzintra's illness as scarlet fever, and she had been rushed to the hospital, the Catholic sister had said it. "We shall need to cut off your child's braids. We are overworked here. Long hair is a bother to care for, and in sickness very unsanitary. To shear is the rule."

Dzintra had quavered, "My father will be sorry." And Mamina had begged of the sister, "Wait, please. Wait another day."

Back at the camp, she told Edvarts. He did not waste a minute. "I'll borrow the Pole's bicycle, and streak off to the hospital," he announced, his mouth grim and determined. On his return that evening he gave his account.

"At the hospital I said to the sister, 'Forgive me, Lady, but it is about my daughter's braids that I come so fast. I would not bother you except that now we are alarmed by the danger from your scissors. You see, in Latvia, braids are traditional young beauty, as with Laima, our goddess of beauty and health. And our own little daughter's golden braids—did it not take eight patient years for them to grow? What a sad waste of time, then, if they are cut off! Lady, if you would but close your eyes for a moment and think, you would see those eight years of our love and pride in our small one's beauty, and how her braids complete her as a Latvian child, whole and perfect. Lady, we keep them, please? You will not cut?'

"The sister did indeed close her eyes," Edvarts continued, "but more in weariness with me than to follow my suggestion. But when she opened them, I saw how they were dancing with a gentle merriment. And she said, 'Herr Darzins, there shall be no cutting of braids if you are willing to have your child not so sanitary. The responsibility of them will be yours.'

"And when I had thanked her, I hastened to tell Dzintra that she need not fear the hospital scissors. I think the child will sleep better tonight."

When Dzintra had almost recovered from the fever, she caught whooping cough from a new little patient. Mamina couldn't endure having her in the disease-ridden hospital a moment longer. "But what can we do when no contagious illness is tolerated in the camp?" fretted Edvarts.

"There is a tiny empty hut just outside the camp," explained Mamina. "Today Astra and I left Janis with Zaiga, and we explored the hut. Once it must have been a storage shed. The dirt floor is strewn with empty cans and bottles, old straw, scraps of dirty paper, wood splinters, bits of coal, even some rotten potatoes."

"There is everything in that hut, and there is nothing," Astra added. "Tevs, the hut is dreadful."

"When it is cleaned, it will not be worse than this terrible camp crowded with every race and breed of men and bedbugs, and not so bad for Dzintra and me as the room we now share indecently with twenty-five others," argued Mamina. "We shall make sack mattresses of clean straw. Tevs will make us a cooking grill, like those the refugees in this camp have contrived from tin cans. A box will serve as a table. Our silver knives and forks from Latvia will remind us to keep our chins up. Now it is summer, and the hut requires no heat. There I shall nurse Dzintra through the whooping cough. She will no longer be homesick for me. And when Janis is carried to the door, she will see for herself that he is still with us. At night Tevs will guard our safety. You, Astra, and Zaiga will stay at camp and care for Janis."

Since the hut stood out of bounds, and Mamina had left of her own accord, there was the question of food. "Fresh vegetables and fruit—how good they would be for my Dzintra!" sighed Mamina. She sent for the *kundze* Zilava. "Let us tramp into the country," she proposed, "to buy milk and garden stuff for our children."

"We must never go on Mondays or Tuesdays," answered the *kundze*. "I have seen hungry Germans from the cities, also the black marketeers, hurl themselves on the packed Sunday trains, then swarm all over the countryside after food. They must surely strip the farms bare."

So the two women selected better days. "To think of the brimming pails I used to carry in from the cow stables at home!" said Mamina, trudging the roads. "I, too," mourned *Kundze* Zilava. They talked about their good brown cows as lovingly as of their old neighbors.

Edvarts and Astra knew it meant shame for Mamina to creep like a beggar from house to house. Although, when her back did not ache too much, she laughed as she told them how the farmers rumbled like ogres from behind their locked doors. "Who is there? I have nothing to sell. No milk."

"Any fresh asparagus, then? Any sauerkraut in brine?" Mamina would inquire bravely of the door front.

"Go away. Nothing."

"Any plums? Any pears? Any apples?" squeaked Mamina, craven within, bold without. "Herr Farmer, I can pay with American cigarettes, given my husband for his guard work in DP camp."

She would wait, and as often as not be obliged to sneak off, unanswered and empty-handed. But again, through a crack in the door, the farmer would growl, "For the cigarettes I trade a dozen or so apples."

So, in Dzintra's illness and the family separation, the Darzins once more placed their "sorrow under a stone," as in the folk song. And if they did not "skip over it, singing," they managed to limp over it without whimpering.

In time, the hospital with its ill and dying children, the miserable camp seething with its mixed nationalities and endless jargon, the poor hideaway hut, became but harsh memories. For now it was late summer of 1946, and the Darzins were in a new camp, in a city on the Neckar River, called Esslingen. Last October they had come eagerly to it, because they had heard it was all-Latvian. "Thousands of us are here," said Astra. "Perhaps we shall see some people we used to know, friends who knew Marga and our home in Vidzeme."

When Edvarts took his family to be registered at the camp office, he made a point of asking a question himself. "Please, is there one registered here by the name of Eriks Baltais?"

But a search through the files by the office worker brought the answer, "No one here by that name."

When the Latvian interpreter asked about Janis, Mamina answered, "We tell the truth. The child is not ours. We do not know his surname, nor his exact age." Mamina felt, rather than saw, Dzintra's wide, anxious gaze. She went on, firmly. "But Janis is our own, please, unless his father claims him." Mamina then told the baby's brief story. Joy blazed up within Dzintra when she saw his name recorded as Janis Darzins, even though a question mark followed the entry. On the way back to their quarters, Edvarts murmured, "The little oldmother—maybe she should not feel so strongly about the Janiti."

Astra heard him, and later, over the baby's box-crib, she warned Dzintra. "Try not to love Janiti so much, sister. If you must give him up to his father some day, it will hurt."

Dzintra's heart quivered. A quiver ran over her face. She slipped her finger under the curl which graced the baby's topknot. "This curl is like a sweet little gold feather," she said, quietly.

So the Darzins settled among the Latvian exiles clustered thickly in that part of Esslingen called "the old city." More and more came, until the camp became one of the largest in Europe. In the woods above the town, in big brick barracks formerly housing German soldiers, lived the Latvian old, the ailing, the single men and women, and couples having pre-school children. The pure air and the quiet, the charming views of town and winding river were healing to those wanderers not too desperately afflicted with homesickness and despair. Amid these barracks were also the American executive offices. Astra and Dzintra thought the hills surrounding Esslingen were beautiful, for they were fringed with climbing terraces in a bright mosaic of fields, gardens and vineyards. The aroma of ripe grapes drifted down. The wine-makers were busy.

The Darzins were one of many families alloted a room in an apartment building. "I can't help feeling guilty, pushing out the Germans who lived here," sighed Mamina.

"It is the way things are," declared Edvarts with finality. "The American government has arranged it for us homeless ones."

Some of the displaced ate in the camp dining rooms. Others stood in line for the ready-cooked food and carried it to their rooms. Some bought the raw provisions from the commissary. "That is what we shall do," Mamina decided. "If we cook and eat by ourselves, it will seem more like home." In the kitchen shared with three other families, Mamina and Astra awaited their turn to cook. There was a gas stove, which was rare. The German woman who had been forced out, dearly loved that stove. More than once she returned to look at it, her eyes hot with jealousy. She said, "The American government promises the return of this apartment when you leave, and God speed that day. In the meantime, you will treat the stove well?"

"I'll watch that no harm comes," promised Mamina.

The European displaced persons' camps furnished food, shelter, clothing and medical care. The diet was more ample and nourishing than the native Germans were able to provide for themselves. Yet it was monotonous, especially in winter. "Soup, soup, corn! Never do I want to see another can of corn!" complained Astra, half laughing. In their dreams the refugees all but chewed and swallowed juicy mutton, pink slices of veal, red beefsteaks, chops and sausages. For as time went on, and the Germans were obliged to kill their cattle to feed themselves, fresh meat and milk became more scarce.

"At least we do not need food cards to buy flowers," said Astra, bringing bouquets from the booths in the Marktplatz.

"Nē," agreed Mamina. "Though we are poor, we shall have flowers in our window."

In Esslingen's "old city," a large German school building had been taken over for the use of the camp. Dzintra was placed in the second grade, Astra in high school. She and Dzintra were happy because their friend Zaiga Kimenis was among the large number of excellent Latvian teachers.

Edvarts Darzins was a camp councilor. Displaced persons who worked for the good of the camp, councilors, teachers, doctors, nurses, police, cooks, seamstresses, carpenters—all were rewarded not with coin, but with cigarettes, which were always exchangeable in trade. Zaiga organized three Girl Scout troops at Esslingen, and others in smaller camps nearby. Mamina helped when she could.

"Oh, I wish I weren't getting so *old!*" wailed sixteen-year-old Astra. "I can't be a Girl Scout much longer." During the past summer she had helped with the younger troops, of which Dzintra was a member. There had been swimming in the lake, hikes and picnics along the Neckar River and among the hills.

A stocky young Texan acted as the American welfare director. Her name was Sybil Grant. "I'm far from the *sibyl* type," she laughed. "Call me Bluebonnet. That's the Texas flower. Bluebonnet doesn't describe me, either, not with these muscles. But I'm sentimental about my state. It's over ten times bigger than Latvia," she boasted, in the Texas-proud way. No one minded. Bluebonnet's smile was so wide and winning. When she walked through the Old City, or clattered up to the hill camp in a jeep, the children ran laughing to meet her. The women kissed her hands. Courtly and smiling, the men bowed to her.

"Did you ever read a book called *The Secret Garden?*" Dzintra inquired of Bluebonnet.

"In my tenth year I slept with it every night," answered the Texan, grinning. "Astra, it's fine you can read English. Maybe next year I can get you a job in one of the headquarters offices. Do you happen to type?"

"I'm learning in high school, now." Astra flushed with pleasure.

Upon hearing the story of Janis, Bluebonnet declared

that his father could be traced if he were in any of the zonal camps.

Dzintra could not cry out in protest, as she longed to do. Her parents had said it was wicked of her to hope that the baby's father would never appear. But at least she could point out an important fact. "None of us ever learned his name, Miss Bluebonnet."

"Phooey!" exclaimed the welfare director, not realizing how much Dzintra cared. "Grubbing up a guy who was formerly a musician of Riga would be easy!"

Then I wish I could hide the baby, thought Dzintra. *I could hide him in the little attic space assigned to us on the top floor of our apartment building.*

But this was only a very secret wish. In the meantime the camp councilors sought a conference with Miss Grant. "Many of our people are occupied here," they pointed out, "although so differently than at home. Often the work seems dull and futile to them. They need more entertainment to liven them up."

Bluebonnet heartily agreed. In Esslingen Camp news went around that there would be more general folk-singing. The old folk dances would be taught to the youngsters who had never known them. Groups would perform for the pleasure of all. Dzintra imagined herself a sail, whirling round and round in the windmill dance. Astra's toes tingled. Ah, but she remembered the dancing classes at her old school, and stepping out the measures with Marga or Rolands on St. John's Eve!

While Bluebonnet breezed around, encouraging, she also did a little scolding. "It's a fact," she said, "that hardship brings out the best in some and the worst in others. While some of you work cheerfully for the good of the camp, others are gloomy shirkers. Some of you cling to a steady faith that a better day is coming for you and your families. Others brood desperately over thoughts of poison or a rope around the neck. You gripe about standing in line for handouts of clothing. You whine about the tiresome questioning and the filling out of forms at the office."

Bluebonnet choked up, but after a moment she went on. "*Wait, hope, homesickness, despair*—oh, I understand that endless round. I know you've suffered terribly. You've lost everything but your lives. But you have gained the compassion of the western world, now pouring out its money and gifts for you. I'm thrilled to my soul when I think of this beautiful reaching out of nations in Christian charity."

It would have been preaching from anyone else. But not from Bluebonnet Grant, who was thoroughly selfless and kind, and who must not, therefore, hear any more whining from Esslingen Camp.

Astra and Dzintra were proud when their father was elected to prepare a handicraft exhibit. It was to be on the second floor of a building in the old town which was already in use by the camp. In this building, and in the immense barn behind it, were sewing machines and looms, potters' wheels and forges, work benches and tools. Edvarts promised that everyone would work hard to have the exhibit ready by spring. Bluebonnet declared that Americans would come to see it and to buy.

With great care, Edvarts made a handsome sign to go

above the entrance to the display—*Latviesu Dailamat-niecība*. But the English translation, Latvian Art Handicraft, must appear on the same sign. How Edvarts fretted over those strange words! It took Astra, Zaiga Kimenis, and finally Texas Bluebonnet to inspire him with enough courage to complete the sign.

So that winter was far less dull than the preceding one. In the late spring, just after the handicraft exhibit was opened, a newcomer to the camp surprised the Darzins family, and was himself surprised. He might never have come had not something else happened first. It happened early in 1947, while it was still winter.

16   ON THE CASTLE STAIRS

In the snow, through Esslingen Camp, Astra and her mother went begging. Zaiga Kimenis went in her free time. The *kundze* Zilava not only begged but demanded. Other Latvian women, even the old watchmaker's wife, begged. It was a matter of patriotism and the heart's deep sympathy.

"Can you spare a man's coat?" Astra pled of those who answered her knock in the "old town" camp, or in the barracks atop the snowy hill. "Could you give a pair of trousers, or a shirt?" Although the need was so urgent, Astra was likely to laugh a little. The requests were outrageous. Everyone agreed. "Why, we have scarcely enough to cover our own backs," the people groaned, gazing at this pretty young beggar at the door.

"I know," she answered patiently. "But just the other day we all queued up for a new distribution of American clothing. Perhaps that other coat you had—could you give that coat?"

"Jā, we give. We give what we can. Here, take it quickly."

At last there was enough to fill a truck. In the night it went out secretly, a truckload of sacrifice and fervent prayers. One of the camp councilors drove. Pastor Jansons went along, wearing his seedy clerical coat and hat. His thin face shone with goodness. His voice was gentle, yet resolute. Jā, he was the one to talk to the British officer at the prison barracks.

Esslingen Camp was tense with waiting when Pastor Jansons came back and reported. "What I said to the British officer went something like this. 'Sir, you hold many of our Latvian soldiers imprisoned here. To you they are the same as your German war enemies. But to us—well, they are the same as we are—victims of war and dispersal. We hear that you are turning these men over to the Russians, who were your war allies. But perhaps, also, you do that because you wish to be rid of them. We hear that some of these prisoners have killed themselves rather than be delivered to the Reds. Sir, at great sacrifice to many Latvian exiles, we have brought a truckload of civilian clothes. Will you accept them for our countrymen?'

"Of course," the pastor went on, smiling wanly, for his night errand had been an ordeal, "I could not come right out and say that we hoped the prisoners could escape in the civilian clothes. But the officer understood perfectly. He answered, 'The prisoners here are good chaps. I do not like the suicides. You may talk with the men. You may leave the clothes. I will turn my back to escapes I do not actually witness."

So that was the thing which happened in the winter, and news filtered back to Esslingen that many of the prisoners had indeed escaped in the donated clothing. Somewhere in Germany they now mingled with the hordes of other exiles.

Early spring came, and late spring, and the day of the grand opening of the Art Handicraft Exhibit. An accordionist strolled through the rooms, playing Baltic airs. Flowers were everywhere. Edvarts was excited and proud. Mamina served as one of the saleswomen, wearing a festival costume she had contrived, and over it her mother's exquisite shawl. The Latvians yearned for the beautiful things which few of them could buy. Americans and British came to admire and to purchase the hand-woven linens, the carved wood, the gleaming brown pottery, the tooled leather work, the costume dolls. Edvarts had never made more beautiful jewelry. In the evening the young men and women performed the folk dances. "Lovely! Wonderful!" Spurred by the applause and the special praise of Bluebonnet Grant, Astra and her young companions danced until they were out of breath.

In the meantime, there were lessons. At the end of each school day, Dzintra rushed home to assure herself that Janis' father had not come during her absence and taken away his little son forever. Generally she found the baby peacefully sleeping. "He is beautiful, Mamina," she would crow.

"*Jā,*" agreed Mamina, "and he is like our own. But remember, child, that perhaps we may keep him only for a while."

Dzintra's lips tightened. She would never say such words, even to herself.

One afternoon, having taken her usual reassuring peek at the sleeping baby, she begged of Astra, "This is just the kind of day to climb to the hills."

"Go, and enjoy yourselves," urged Mamina. "The days are so much longer now, and if you come home immediately afterward, you may stop in the market square to watch the march of the twelve apostles during the six o'clock carillon."

"We shall bring you some wild flowers, Mamina," promised Astra. "Sister, let's take the open paths up the hills, and come back by way of the castle stairs."

The girls made the steep climb slowly. Birds sang to them from tree and bush and grassy thicket. There were wild flowers to gather and to talk about. At the summit stood what was left of the old citadel. From its base the girls could look down into the valley, and see the chimneys and closely clustered terra-cotta roofs of Esslingen. The tall spire of Frauenkirchen Church, with its intricate fretted carvings, reminded Dzintra of some of her father's handworked jewelry. Treetops were delicately budding. Gardens lay along the winding river that reflected the blue of the sky. "The pastor says this is an ancient city," said Astra, pointing. "Down there, and there again, you may see the remains of the stone walls which once fortified it. It is strange that we are here, who were never born here," she mused.

"What would we be doing in Latvia on a day like this, sister?"

"We would have taken the cows to pasture, dear Brune and the others. We would be digging and hoeing the brown earth—our own Latvian earth," answered Astra, dreamily. "The larks would be fluttering up from the flowery meadows, and their song dropping down from the high air like golden stars. The sweet breath of the pines would make us scarcely able to bear our happiness. We should have to close our eyes against the sparkle of the lake. We should be making gay talk with Redlegs and his wife. At noon we should have milk and rye bread, new lettuce dressed with dill and sour cream, homemade cheese, and oh—just naming the good things makes my poor stomach groan! After dinner we would spread our blankets in the orchard. The bees would hum us to sleep. *Lellite,* please try to remember."

"I remember my apple tree," answered Dzintra, slowly, "and the doll I buried, poor thing! Brune and the storks I remember. That time when Cousin Eriks came in the night—I think I remember him. Vecmamina and Uncle Imants, and Mikelis who rode me on his shoulder, *jā!* And, of course, Ruta and the good smells from her cooking kettles. But oh, I wish I could remember my grandmother who pledged me her *sakta!* I wish I could remember my own sister Marga."

"You were so young when Marga said good-bye that was good-bye forever. But you look like her, *lellite.* It

makes us glad that she seems to live again in you. . . .
But now I shall sing you a Latvian song which matches
this bright day, and what we are doing in Germany this
minute:"

> "Singing I climbed the hill
> White with clover.
> May my beautiful songs
> Pour into the clover leaves."

"Always with us Latvians it is singing. And this,
lellite, is a folk song of love and beauty that is beyond
you. But I am sixteen. So I shall sing it." Astra's
laughter pealed out, making gay fun of herself, romanc-
ing:

> "I grew like a slender linden,
> Beautiful as a cinnamon flower.
> And enticed the strangers' lads
> From a hundred miles away."

Astra caught Dzintra's hand. "Now we must fly down
the castle stairs, if we are to see the parade of the twelve
apostles at six o'clock. Besides, our flowers will wither
before ever we can give them to Mamina."

But the girls could not fly. They had to watch their
footing. Hollows and broken edges were worn into the
treads of the castle stairs. They were black with age.
Ancient-black was the thick wooden wall built against
the hillside. It supported the structure. Ancient-black
were the great oaken beams holding up the broken roof.
The broad hand-rail was polished to a silvery gloss from
the rub of many fingers. Once Dzintra and Astra had

counted the steps as they mounted. There were six hundred and two. Standing at the base, looking up, the stairs seemed to dwindle to a narrow channel of darkness, and there, as the girls knew, turned sharply as they led to the castle.

"Anything could happen on these ghostly old stairs," observed Astra. "If they could talk, what stories they might tell!"

Dzintra, tripping downward, had been gazing out the open side of the stairs at the sunlit valley. But now she turned in merriment as she listened to Astra. "Let's pretend," she said, "that this fellow mounting the steps is the lord of the castle as it was in its proud days. Or, he could be one of those strangers' lads coming one hundred miles because he has heard of your far-famed beauty."

"Whether he is lord or not, I shall not even look at him." Astra laughed.

But when the moment came, her glance stole sidewise toward the dark, unhappy face of the boy passing by on the stairs. She went on, but three steps down she halted. All her childhood days of play and school seemed to rush headlong into her mind. Quickly, then, she turned to look up at the stranger. He had also stopped, and was staring at her.

"Rolands!" breathed Astra. "Surely you are my old schoolmate, Rolands Kruze!"

"Marga Darzins!" whispered the boy, coming down five steps. "But *nē*, not poor Marga! You are Astra!" Joy flickered over his face, but as if it were a light which could not stay. "Astra Darzins! At Easter we used to swing together. On St. John's Eve we danced together. At school we played the game of 'Colors.' You are older. You are much taller. But I would have recognized you anywhere. Do you know, you are the first person from home that I've seen?"

"Are you registered in Esslingen Camp as a displaced person?" Astra inquired.

Rolands stole a cautious look around, as if the ancient stairs had not only ears, but a tongue to tell tales on him. Despair settled again on his thin face. "I am not registered. I'm afraid to try. My war record may bar me. The Americans might send me to prison."

Astra looked at Rolands inquiringly. He went on. "I was in that British camp to which the Esslingen Latvians sent clothing. I escaped, wearing my allotment, although I soon sold the coat for food. I managed to find work among the Germans. I was one of a gang cleaning war rubble in Mannheim. I worked in a cheese factory in Kempten. But all the time I dreamed of coming here. Three days ago I did it. But I've only been wandering the streets, eating out of my pocket, afraid of naming myself as a former draftee of the German Army, afraid of—well, I've been terribly despondent, not knowing what is to become of me. A moment ago a kind of blind desperation drove me up these steps to the ruins above. I was going to—"

"Oh, Rolands!" cried Astra. "The will to live and to hope is like a banner which we must carry and never let fall. Come home with me, now. My parents will be so pleased to see you. This is my sister Dzintra."

"When I first saw you, I was afraid you might be Janis' father," confessed Dzintra, smiling.

Rolands disregarded this remark, for it meant nothing to him. *"Dzintarzeme*—Amberland," he mused, looking at Dzintra with pleasure. "Little one, you are true amber, like Marga. I used to think Marga was the most beautiful girl anywhere." Rolands turned to gaze at Astra, but as if he saw her from a long way off. *"Jā,* Marga was beautiful, but sisters can be beautiful, differently."

Astra answered with a laugh, trying to lighten Rolands' spirits. "A gallant little speech, Rolands, but I shall never be half as pretty as dear Marga." In spite of the pang she felt at talking of Marga with some one who had known her well, why was she suddenly more pleased with Rolands' compliment than any she had ever received?

"If you are afraid, Rolands," Dzintra spoke up, "and do not want an American camp worker like Bluebonnet Grant to see you, you could hide in the little attic space allotted to us." She said it rather carelessly. Yet Astra thought how clever it was of her young sister to understand Rolands' problem. The child went on. "Now let's not stand here forever, or we shall miss the carillon."

In the Marktplatz there were others pausing to listen to the bells chiming out the evening hymn. The door at the base of the great clock opened. On their revolving platform the carved wooden figures of the twelve apostles appeared, one by one, to circle slowly, solemnly, and disappear as the last note struck.

"They are old—those dear little apostles!" Dzintra

sighed with pleasure. "How weary they must be of marching out three times a day, year after year! Yet they are holy men. They never tire of doing their duty."

At the door of the apartment building where the girls lived, Rolands hesitated. "Ever since I came to Esslingen, and long before, there is something I have yearned to know. Perhaps my mother—do you know, Astra, whether she is in this camp?"

To Astra came the very smell of that rainy night in Riga Harbor, the very sound of that long cry, that deep splash. *The poor kundze Kruze—after all, she cannot go!* *Nē*, this was not the moment to tell Rolands the fate of his mother.

She caught his hand. "Come," she cried, pretending gaiety. "I can't wait to show Tevs and Mamina what Dzintra and I found on the castle stairs—*you!*"

17   ASTRA AND ROLANDS

It was the Darzins' week to clean the hall and stairway
in their part of the apartment building. This morning
Astra and Dzintra had been sweeping and mopping.
When they had finished and tidied themselves, Dzintra
bumped the baby's cart down the steps to the street.
Astra followed, carrying him. "Let's take Janiti along
the river walk," suggested Dzintra, "where many people
go."

"What a show-off is our little oldmother!" teased
Astra.

"Jā." Dzintra frankly admitted it. "But Janiti brings
light to the saddest face. All who pass stop to admire

him. It is a joke, Astra, but so-o nice, when they say to
me, 'What a winsome child is your infant brother!' "

Astra smiled. She knew that the passers-by were quite
as attracted to Dzintra's golden charm and her shining
pride in the baby. But this morning, walking with
Dzintra by the riverside, Astra had little to say. The
sight of the water, flowing placidly by, did not cool her
thoughts, nor did the beauty of summer leaf-shadows on
the path calm her.

"You hear nothing, sister," complained Dzintra. "You
do not answer me."

"It is Rolands who troubles me so!" Astra exclaimed.
"He should take Tevs' advice and present himself at
headquarters. The longer he waits to apply as a displacee, the worse it will be for him, and the more he will
have to explain. For a month now he roams the streets.
For a month he sleeps in our attic cubby. For a month
now, because he has no right to a food card, we share
with him, and so do the other eighty-five people in our
apartment building."

"He is welcome," said Dzintra, always kind. "For
many to share with one Latvian soldier is hard on no
one, Mamina says."

"Of course he is welcome!" cried Astra. "And he is
welcome to the new shirt Mamina made for him, and
the coat that Pastor Jansons got for him. But all this
taking without giving—it is bad for Rolands. This decep-
tion of hiding from the American authorities—oh, it is
dreadfully bad for him! He should face his danger
squarely, and act. Tevs tells him that. I tell him, until
at last I can say no more. He thinks I do not understand

what he is up against. That makes me so unhappy."
Astra's voice dropped to a whisper.

"I can tell, sister," said Dzintra, "that Rolands wants
you, more than anyone else, to think well of him."

That evening, after an early supper, Astra left the
apartment to visit a girl friend she had made at the camp
high school. But on the way, she saw Rolands Kruze
coming toward her. He was pale. His hair was tousled.
But he wore a new air of resolution. "I want to tell you,"
he said, "that tomorrow I am going to make application
as a displaced person."

"Oh, Rolands, I am so glad!" cried Astra.

"Glad? I may be rejected. Then I shall either become
a wanderer in this overcrowded land, or find myself
behind prison walls. Nē, Astra, I am only being a little
sarcastic about your gladness. All day I have been struggling with myself. Thinking of my poor mother and
sister, I asked myself why I should go on living in a world
full of such greed and struggle, such cruelty and fear.
Everybody afraid of something or some one! And my
own particular problem! I would rather face the guns of
battle than walk into the American headquarters and
take all that questioning. Jā," confessed Rolands, "I was
about to beat my head to a pulp against the ruined tower
on the hill. Astra, I know that you think of me as a
coward."

"My heart does not call you a coward. Who am I to
call any of our unhappy people that?" answered Astra.
"But my father has heard that the Americans are to take
a census of this camp. So you would either have to skip
out before that, or be caught as an unregistered person.

Tevs says that your chances of being accepted here are good. Weren't you drafted into the German Army when you were only sixteen, and remained a common soldier throughout the war?"

"Thank Heaven, I was never branded with the SS tattoo!" Rolands said. "That would have been fatal for me, as the Americans would have taken it as certain evidence that I was a Nazi."

"Think of it, Rolands! If you are accepted here, you can finish high school in the camp. Oh, it will be wonderful to see you hold up your head and not go sneaking about, afraid of being discovered! And when Latvia becomes a free nation once more, you can return in safety." Astra's voice dropped. "If it is never freed in our time, then perhaps there will be some honorable course for us. But surely you have had no supper. I was on my way to see my girl friend, but I will go back to the apartment with you. Rolands," she cried, gaily, "did you know that tomorrow is my name day?"

"The traditional name-day cake for our Astra!" cried Mamina, the next evening, while her family and Rolands stared in astonishment. "*Nē*, it was not easy to put together, far from the eggs and the potato yeast of our Vidzeme kitchen! Where to get the saffron to make the dough yellow, and where the chopped nuts to bake with sugar in the crust!"

"Yet here is the cake, whole and perfect!" Astra's voice quavered with more than laughter. "Mamina, you work miracles!"

"It was a miracle from heaven," declared Mamina.

"Listen! Yesterday you thought our fresh flowers came as usual from the booth in the Marktplatz. But not so. For there came a German woman knocking at our door. 'I am Frau Hermerding,' she said. 'Always as I pass I see flowers in your window. And I think to myself that behind the window is a woman who is like me in her love of flowers. Therefore she cannot be a stranger. So I have brought you something from my garden.' With that she handed me the bouquet. *Jā*," admitted Mamina, "for a moment I could not see the flowers for tears.

"I invited the Frau inside, and we talked. She said to me, 'Oh, but I know about your country! My husband was with the German Army in Latvia and shipped me much food from there. *Himmel*, Latvia must be very rich, with all that food to spare! The eggs he sent I preserved in water glass. Lucky I am to have eggs, *ja?*'"

Mamina waved her hands dramatically. "Imagine hearing from the Frau's own lips that she has layers and layers of Latvian eggs which we had to give until we had none for ourselves! But that Frau—she was so pleased, and so astonishingly dense! *Nē*, I could not be resentful. Instead—now, don't laugh—I felt drawn to her because her cellar holds richness straight from our dear homeland. Also, there was her gift of flowers."

"So then?" asked Dzintra, eagerly, and indeed all the Darzins were hanging on Mamina's story.

"So then I told Frau Hermerding about our farm in Latvia. I told her about you, Dzintra, and the amber in your name, and how baby Janis was left in your lap. I told about Marga. I told about Astra and how today her name-day cake must be only a sad makeshift. With gestures and words I pictured how in Latvia the cake would be beautiful, twisted in rings like the figure eight, a candle in each ring, and flowers all around.

"The Frau said that she always keeps a brewing of potato yeast, and she would give me a start. She thought she had a sprinkling of saffron powder. *Jā*, she was kind! So I mustered up my courage. I said to her, 'My husband is lately a little rich because Miss Grant, the American welfare worker, paid him for a hand-made silver ring. Frau Hermerding, if you would allow me to buy two eggs for the name-day cake! Latvian eggs! What a happy home feeling they would give my family!'

"Frau Hermerding set her jaw. 'I have never sold or given away a single precious egg' she declared, 'and myself, I eat them sparingly. Too,' she pointed out, 'the Latvian eggs are a memorial to my husband, who has never returned, so that I do not know if I am still a wife, or only a widow.'

"However," finished Mamina, triumphantly, "when I took Janis and went with Frau Hermerding to get the yeast and saffron, she sold me two eggs, because, as she explained, 'You made my heart soft when you talked so bravely of your lost daughter Marga.'"

So the Darzins made much of Astra's miraculous name-day cake that tasted of home. They were the more light-hearted because Rolands had made his application that day. His description of the questioning, the filling out of forms and the medical examination was an old story to them. "It may be weeks before I know for sure," sighed Rolands, weary after the gruelling hours.

"Hope, and have patience," Edvarts encouraged him.

"In the meantime you have told the truth. You will be allowed to live openly in the camp. You are allowed your own food card. You have permission to enter high school next month."

"I am almost nineteen, an old man for a third-year student," groaned Rolands.

"On account of having to leave Latvia, most of us are behind in our education," Astra assured him. "And you are smart, Rolands. I remember you could run faster than anyone in our game of 'Colors.' And I can see you now, capering about in neighbor Bracs' harvest-field as the god Jumis."

"Girl, do you believe my brains to be in my feet?" laughed Rolands.

So Rolands went to live in the hilltop barracks, from which he trudged daily to the schoolhouse. He worked hard at his studies, trying to make up for lost time. He was allotted an American suit, a little too small; shoes that pinched slightly; a sweater which he fondly cherished. At night he attended a class in photography. He made friends. He was asked to join a folk-dancing group. He and Astra began pairing together as they took their positions. And while Rolands danced, with the worry about his application always at his heart, the Esslingen Camp audiences made admiring comments. "That tall young Rolands with the deep, troubled eyes, that fair Astra with the pretty figure—with what ease they step and whirl together! *Jā*, that pair is our favorite."

In the winter Dzintra caught measles, then epidemic in the camp. She was sent to the hospital. When she

returned to the apartment it was December. "Baby, how
you have grown!" she cried, smothering Janis with kisses.

"Baby?" questioned Mamina. "According to what his
father told us on the freight train, Janis is about three
years old. He is able to say anything."

"Tevs loves him as he would his own Janiti," declared
Dzintra with satisfaction.

"And now I have come to feel that Janis' father will
never appear," said Mamina. "Something must have
happened to him. After all this time, had he been per-
sistent, he would surely have come to Esslingen."

"But there are about six thousand Latvian displacees
here," Astra reminded her mother.

"Jā, but the Americans have records of us all," Mamina
rejoined. "You know there is a new organization now,
called IRO, which Tevs says works better for us than
the old UNRAA. Through IRO, which is short for
International Refugee Organization, the western nations
are to offer eligible displaced persons new homes and
citizenship. Charity and church leaders are now in the
camp to look us over and offer sponsorship. Already
Latvians are leaving here."

"My girl friend left with her family for the port of
Bremerhaven today. They take ship for South America."

"South America—how far and exciting it sounds!" exclaimed Dzintra. "But I am going back home to our
house and orchard when Latvia is free again. I shall dig
up my *lellite*, but only to be merciful, for now I am
eleven, and too old for dolls. Besides, I have Janiti."

In January Rolands fairly blew into the apartment.
"Now I walk on air!" he cried. "The American Intelli-

gence Corps has cleared me of all suspicion. My papers are in order. At last I am a full-fledged displacee at Esslingen Camp. The minute I was notified, I stopped in that photography shop which I have often passed. I got a part-time job there. The pay is small, but the experience will be wonderful."

So there was a general rejoicing for Rolands' sake, and a special one when he caught Astra and whirled her merrily around the room. Then Mamina made an announcement. "I also have obtained work, sewing for a German modiste who owned a flourishing business before the war, and now designs for the American ladies here." Carefully Mamina unwrapped and displayed a partially completed frock.

"Think of owning and wearing such a lovely gown!" sighed Astra. She laughed. "Mamina, you are one for springing surprises!"

"It will be nice," answered Mamina, demurely, "to have a little money should we go to another country."

"Esslingen Camp is seething with talk," Edvarts told his family. "It is believed that there is no prospect of the Soviet Iron Curtain ever lifting from our country. So now the camp people talk of Australia and of South America. They talk of England and Belgium and Canada. But mostly they talk of the United States. There, opportunities are many, and money is easy. We shall become millionaires in no time at all. But others say, 'We are Europeans. Our dread of leaving European shores is unbearable. It seems as final as doomsday.' "

"Jā, the poor heart weeps," sympathized Mamina. "As for all that talk about becoming millionaires—bah! Perhaps there are a few of the world's poor even in America. We shall need to work, and our pride and our spiritual growth be all the stronger. Of the free countries, though," said Mamina, "I myself would choose the United States. All are equal there. We would not be looked down upon because we are DP's and poor."

June of 1948 brought scholarship honors to both Astra and Rolands. The camp raised a small fund, and three teachers took them and eight other honor students on a jaunt to Garmisch-Partenkirchen, twin villages in the Bavarian Alps. It was a sparkling morning when they traveled to Munich, where they changed trains. Watching eagerly for a first sight of the mountains, the students saw them as a haze of blue cloud, then looming up as a giant wall. In high country the railway ended. The young travelers went on by bus, past lakes, fir-clad slopes, lush meadows and scattered gabled villages, the summits towering directly above. There was a change to electric train. It ran through deep clefts and tunnels.

"These are my first mountains," said Astra, her voice tight with excitement. "Aren't they gorgeous?"

"This excursion is great fun," Rolands agreed. "And here we are at the twin villages. Look at the mountains now, all bare rock and gleaming glacier."

One of the teachers spoke. "See the one which rises above all others. It is the highest in Germany. We are to be carried up there in a steel basket. Who wishes to go on the first trip?"

Astra stepped forward, her eyes sparkling. Rolands was close behind her. Three other students and a teacher quickly followed. Presently they were swinging in the basket through incredible space, up, up, and up. Yet their eyes turned more often toward earth, far below, as they gasped and shivered, and closed their eyes dizzily, only to open them again, and laugh a little. Now the hamper stopped, hanging motionless. What had happened? The students were frightened. Chills prickled their scalps. But with a reassuring mutter, and as calmly as if he were but two feet from the valley floor instead of thousands, the operator climbed to the mechanism above the swinging basket. He did some tinkering, then descended and resumed his place. The basket sailed on and up.

The afternoon was spent in hiking. It was rough going among the rocks, and there were cushions of moss into which the young climbers found their feet sinking ankle-deep, and sometimes to the knee. They went slowly as a matter of good sense. Often they stopped to admire the scenery and to breathe deeply of the thin, invigorating air. Garmisch-Partenkirchen appeared far below as toy villages, and the citizens as tiny, animated dolls. Above and around, the peaks soared majestically dark, their crevices brightened with sun-dazzled snow. The teen-agers rolled snow balls and enjoyed a merry battle, growing red-cheeked and warm with exercise and laughter. The contrast of unmelting snow, hot sun, and the girls' summer dresses seemed odd and amusing. Descending again to the trail, one of the girl students began experimenting with echoes. "Where are we going now?" she called.

"Whe - e - rr go-o-o-ing Nn -OWWW?" It was as if

some over-sized mountain nymph took a far, lonely pleasure in mockery, but in tones more solemn, more strange and bell-like.

A teacher shouted, "We are searching for the lake Eibsee." The long echo rolled back. "I-I-Ibsee-see." And when the students joined together in challenge, a jangle of sound was flung harshly back at them, finally to die away, long-held and ghostly.

The beauty of Eibsee Lake, a gleaming jewel in its high-ringed setting, hushed the young people into silence. Astra and Rolands moved apart from the others to stand entranced. "This is fairyland, and more," whispered Astra, presently. "This is a holy place. If one could be quite alone here, one might actually *see* holiness. . . . Do you feel as I do in this immensity, Rolands, uplifted, yet very small, very common and earthy? The dull years of camp life and our past sufferings seem far away, vanished almost into nothing."

"But you are not common and earthy, Astra," Rolands avowed. "To me you are more rare and precious than anyone. I knew it when I stood there on the castle stairs, and saw your eyes deep with the kindness and understanding I sorely needed. Your eyes are as clear as this mountain lake. They are as blue as these lovely gentians. Astra, after the horrors of war, you seemed to me from the first like a flower. So do I constantly think of you."

Astra turned toward him, pink-cheeked, her eyes suddenly moist. "That is a lovely thing to hear in this lovely place," she answered. Gravely she turned to join the others.

"But what if you go to the United States, and I to Australia, with seas between us?" begged Rolands, trailing her.

"Make your destination Canada, at least." Astra shot him such a mischeivous glance from under her lashes that he had to laugh a little. Then she added, as if in warning, "I am not quite eighteen, Rolands." *And oh, happier at this moment than I have been since Marga and I played together as children. Royally happy!*

"But I am almost twenty," Rolands argued, unaware of her secret joy.

Over her shoulder she teased back at him. *"Twenty,* and still another year of high school, four years of college, five, six, ten years of building up a business. Oldfather, there is a century of growth ahead of you!"

18

THE VIOLIN

December of 1948 had only just begun when one evening Mamina told of an incident she had enjoyed that day. "I met the stove lady in the Platz." Mamina's eyes twinkled, and her family smiled as one, for her stories were invariably entertaining to them.

"The lady is always delighted to see me," related Mamina, "but only because of the opportunity to inquire about the health of the stove. Today she approached the subject both delicately and rudely, saying, 'You will be cooking your Christmas feast, Frau Darzins, on my stove which the United States so highhandedly allowed you.'

"So I decided to become a little rude, too," confessed Mamina, wickedly. "I answered, 'Madam, we have not had a Christmas feast since we lived in Latvia, and then only before the Russians and the Germans and again the Russians took from us everything that made feasting a joy, or even possible. So please do not fret yourself. Your stove will suffer no damage this Christmas from extra cooking.'

" 'News is *gut!*' spat out the stove lady.

" 'I have much better news for you, Madam,' I assured her, although I must say my freezing 'madams' were completely wasted on her," admitted Mamina. " 'Since August, Madam,' I went on, intending to torture her with a little suspense, 'we Darzins have been exchanging letters with the United States. Not the United States on the hill above Esslingen, but the United States across the Atlantic Ocean. Because, Madam, in August our names appeared on the schoolhouse bulletin board. *Come, Edvarts and Kristine Darzins and children, Astra, Dzintra and Janis, to the headquarters office on the hill. The Lutheran Church in the United States of America has acquired two sponsors for you, one of which you may choose in the course of your resettlement routine.* At least, Madam, that's what the notification on the bulletin board really meant.'

"By this time the stove lady was completely spellbound by my storytelling. Indeed, although the noon carillon was sounding, neither of us cast a single glance at the twelve apostles. '*Jā*, Madam,' I continued, 'all is about to be settled for us. We have had still another physical examination at Ludwigsburg. We have an-

swered the million questions for the millionth time. Our
papers are stamped with *this certifies,* and *that certifies.*
They are signed with flourishes. So in three days from
now we take train for Bremen. There we stay in barracks, trembling, while the United States consulate asks
questions all over again. There, in no clothes at all, we
are examined again by the most strict of all American
doctors in Germany. Then, Madam, if we have not been
detected in falsehoods; if we are not found to be too old,
to have smallpox, tuberculosis, or even a stomach-ache,
we are allowed to go to Bremerhaven. An emigrant
transport is there. We file aboard. We sail. We go to
America to a state called Indiana. It has something to
do with Indians. Inside this province stands a city
named Indianapolis. There, a silversmith is to sponsor
and employ my husband. There we settle. *Nē,* Madam,'
I wound up, not having another instant to waste, 'we
shall not be cooking on your precious stove. For at
Christmas time, God and the American consulate helping us, we shall be at sea.' "

"Wife, how you exaggerate!" Edvarts doubled over
with laughter.

"But it is every word true, Tevs!" cried Dzintra.
"Didn't the stove lady ever get what you were driving
at, Mamina?"

"Finally. At last. Suddenly her face became as the
sun in the heavens, blinding me, really blinding me!"
Mamina laughed. " '*Lieber Himmel!*' cried the happy
Hausfrau, 'Maybe at last I get my stove back—my
kitchen, my apartment! This minute I run to the United
States on the hill. Politely I remind of promise. With

praying hands I implore. *Ja,* I get maybe.' Suddenly the madam grasped my arm. 'You will arrange, please, that no DP's dismantle the stove, and carry away pieces to United States?'

"So I promised on my soul that the stove would keep every leg, arm and finger, and the madam hurried away as fast as she could waddle. It would have been nice," observed Mamina, wistfully, "if the stove lady had wished us a safe voyage and a good settlement in the United States. How we need good wishes!" Mamina's lips suddenly trembled. Then she smiled a little.

"It was different from Frau Hermerding, when we exchanged our good-byes. She said she was sorry, that she would miss us. She gave me this jar of plum preserves. In kind farewell she said, 'Whenever I allow myself a Latvian egg, I shall think not only of my husband, but of you, dear Frau Darzins.'"

"Tomorrow I, too, shall say good-bye to the girls and boys at school," Dzintra asserted with a trace of self-importance, "and good-bye to Zaiga Kimenis, my teacher. I wish she were going to America with us."

"Her papers are now going through the office," Astra volunteered. "By March, perhaps, she should be emigrating. Tevs, I am to work up to the last minute before we leave for Bremen. How good it was of Miss Bluebonnet to get me the job of typing! I have felt useful there. And like Mamina at her sewing, I shall have a little money of my own when we reach the place called Indianapolis."

"I have a daughter who works in the American office," boasted Edvarts. "*Jā,* didn't I say that my Astra would be 'piling up gold,' like the bee in our folk song, when she learned the English language?"

Astra laughed, ruefully. "Tevs, dear, I do read English a little. But when I try to speak it—alas, the Americans look completely befuddled, not understanding me. Rolands says—"

"By-the-way, does Rolands plan to stow away on our ship, that he may not lose sight of you?" Edvarts' eyes twinkled.

Astra flushed. But there was laughter on her lips, for even to her, Rolands' young desperation was sometimes a little irritating. "Rolands declares that unless he gets a sponsor in Indianapolis, or within walking distance of me, he doesn't care what happens to him. He might even hand himself over to the Soviets! Of course he is only being a little dramatic. But he is disappointed that so far no Indiana photographer is willing to sponsor him. 'Farmers, farmers, farmers,' he cries, 'farmers are the workers most wanted by the western nations.'"

"Young *kungs* Rolands must forget photography for a while," declared Edvarts, impatiently. "Only by signing up as a farmer can he be admitted to America. True, Rolands was never a farmer. But from six to sixteen he worked on his mother's land."

"I reminded him of our school days in Latvia," said Astra, "for when we children planted and tended the school vegetables, Rolands' plants seemed always to grow largest and finest. The headmaster said even then that Rolands Kruze had a green thumb."

"Rolands should have learned patience by this time. In the United States, after he has fulfilled his agreement with his sponsor and has saved some money, perhaps he will be able to set up a photography shop of his own." Edvarts changed the subject. "Another letter has come to the camp from Pastor Jansons, now in America. His words of encouragement have helped us, nervous and doubtful as we are. 'Come with hope,' writes Pastor Jansons, 'and with determination to enter trustfully into American life. Come resolved to learn the language as soon as possible, for I hear nothing but English in this country, not even German.'

"Ah," groaned Edvarts, "the English language! I can never learn it!"

On their final Sunday at Esslingen Camp the Darzins attended church services, listening to farewell words of advice which the pastor gave out every week, now that family after family were leaving for resettlement in other countries. At the church door many last good-byes were said. *Sveiki*—good-bye—what a common word it had become since the first difficult farewells in Latvia!

That afternoon Astra and Rolands slipped out for a few minutes together. Their feet seemed to turn of themselves toward the castle stairs. Other young couples huddled on the steps, shadowy under the age-blackened roof, while outside the rain fell over hills and valley. Astra and Rolands spoke of their childhood, because *that* they had also shared. "Remember?"—and—"remember?" But they talked chiefly of their unknown future. "We DP's shall be busy in America," said Astra, "busier, perhaps, than we might have been in our own land. I think we may be happy there."

Back at the door of the apartment building, Rolands said what had already been said between them. "You will write, Astra?"

"Of course, Rolands. And you will write me the moment you learn the date of your emigration."

"Astra, you will surely be there when I come, the same girl?"

"A little different, Rolands. For in the meantime I will have experienced a long sea voyage, and beheld the famed Statue of Liberty. I will have seen miles of America from an overland train. I will have learned more American words. I will be on my way toward becoming an American. But *nē*, Rolands, for you I shall be the same Astra, waiting to welcome you when you come."

Two days later, the Darzins arrived in Bremen. They were tense with nervousness. "Now we go through the final crucial tests. Here they are very strict. They see everything. And what if we are found wanting in some way?" Mamina tried to joke a little. "The doctors will pronounce my heart a travel risk. It goes so fast. *Trip, trip, trip!* Fright beats in my throat and wrists and temples."

"Go and lie down, Kristine," advised Edvarts, himself white with anxiety. The girls were pale and quiet. Janis was fretful.

Like flocks of tired migrant birds, hundreds of displaced persons had come to roost for a little while at Bremen. They represented many nationalities, and there was a babel of talk. The men and women lived in separate barracks, meeting at meal time in the common dining hall, or near the bulletin board where crowds were always watching for ship-sailing announcements.

One evening as the Darzins family ate together, Mamina remarked, "On our floor in the women's dormitory there is a voice which torments my memory. 'Whose voice is that?' I ask myself."

"It could belong to someone you knew at Esslingen Camp," suggested Astra.

Mamina shook her head. "*Nē*, it takes me back to Latvia."

"If I were allowed in the women's dormitory," joked Tevs, "I would play secret police, listening and watching. Perhaps I could catch that voice, and set your poor mind at rest."

The very next evening, as Mamina walked with her daughters and Janis along the second-floor corridors, two figures emerged from one of the dormitory rooms. Dzintra noticed the look of amazement and delight that dawned in her mother's eyes.

"Aina! Aina Ekis of Daugavpils!" Mamina cried reaching out her hand in greeting.

Aina flushed with pleasure. "How it warms the heart to see you here, Kristine!" she exclaimed. "You remember the Darzins of Vidzeme, Karina?" Aina turned to her tall daughter, who smiled in quick recognition.

"Karina has grown in inches, as well as in beauty," Mamina complimented. "And Konrads, is he at Bremen, Aina?" The question was cautiously put.

Karina slipped her arm around her mother, for Aina's tears were suddenly flowing.

"Come with us to the dining hall, where we are to meet Edvarts," Mamina urged, gently. "He will be rejoiced to see you. Noisy and crowded as it is there, we can sit together and talk. Our Dzintra and our little Janis came too late in life to remember you. But Astra has never forgotten that day in your house."

Tripping down the stairs hand-in-hand with Karina, Astra felt the same admiration she had experienced nine years ago in Daugavpils. Memories flitted swiftly through her mind—Konrads' music shop; the feast in Aina's pleasant kitchen, three girls in bright native costumes walking through the flag-flying city; the glory of music as free Latvia celebrated its last singing festival; the dreadful shock of the government announcements; the parting at the gates with the Ekis family, the Baltais grandparents, and Eriks.

Karina was remembering, also. "You were ten or eleven then," she said, and her voice had the same remembered gentleness. "I was twelve. Marga was thirteen, and so lovely. Is Marga here?"

Astra shook her head. Then, over their food in the dining hall, the friends exchanged their tragic stories. To save Aina the ordeal, it was Karina who told about her father, Konrads Ekis.

"Mother and I fled by truck from the invading Communists. It carried the women and children, the old and ailing. The men were to follow however they could, and it was agreed that if they did not catch up with us as we fled westward across Latvia, we would wait for them at the seaport of Liepaja. It took us two months to reach Liepaja, for we were constantly dodging the gunfire and bombs of battle. And where it seemed fairly safe, we lingered, hoping that the German troops and our own Latvian soldiers would run the Communists out of our land, so that we could return home. In Liepaja, Mother and I found refuge in the home of a musician friend. Any day my father might come. A month of waiting, and enemy bombs began falling on Liepaja. The musician urged us to delay no longer. He himself was leaving. We came to Germany. About my father, or from him, we have heard never a word."

"Konrads, my friend!" Edvarts' murmur was one of grief and farewell.

But then the conversation lightened. Aina bent on Janis a maternal smile. "The son you always wanted was born to you in Germany?" she asked.

Mamina shook her head. "Let our Dzintra tell Janis' story."

Dzintra was only too happy, and because of her love for the boy, she told his story well. She was inspired by the gasps of astonishment coming from Aina and Karina. In fact, they exchanged such knowing looks and nods, and made such impatient gestures throughout the telling, that Dzintra was obliged to be brief. It was plain that the Ekis pair were bursting with some information.

"Ah, but we have already heard this story!" cried Aina. And Karina echoed, "The very same!"

The Darzins leaned eagerly forward. But not Dzintra. Reaching out, she drew Janis into her lap, because he was falling asleep over his plate, but also because she felt that she was about to lose him. Above his bright curls, she closed her eyes, listening in dread.

Aina began. "Karina and I finally settled in the DP camp at Würzburg. The American welfare director there said that we women refugees could occupy ourselves nobly if we would help in the nearby hospital, especially in cheering those who spoke our language. I offered to go. In the hospital was a young Latvian named Hugo Avots. At first he could move about a little. But he behaved so strangely."

In spite of being in a public dining room, Aina rose from her chair and acted out her next words. "Hugo would start to take a step, then stop, like this, as if paralyzed. '*Kundze*, please, which foot shall I put forward?' he would beg of me, his eyes dark with agony. I would try to guide him. 'Start with this foot, Hugo,' I would advise. 'Lift it from the floor. Forward, now, and set your foot down. Now, the same with the other. Hugo, do not be afraid!' But maybe by that time the poor fellow would be shaking all over, and afterward be deathly sick from nervous strain.

"The doctor explained. 'This young man is by nature highly sensitive. And because he walked many miles over Germany in search of something he could never find, he has a fixed idea that he has lost the simple know-how of walking. He is also seriously ill from grief and malnutrition.'

"The floor nurse told me that when Avots first came to the hospital he would play his violin," Aina continued. "But then he became too weak. Every day he grew weaker.

"Karina often accompanied me to the hospital. She would stand at the foot of Hugo's bed and play for him on his own instrument. Then how soft and rested his eyes would look! One day he whispered that since he did not know the whereabouts of his little son Janis, Karina must keep his violin. He said it would be happy, since she played so well. He told us that he had been a musician in the Riga orchestra."

"Edvarts! Astra! This is astonishing!" gasped Mamina. "Do you hear, Dzintra?"

But Dzintra's head was bent low.

Aina was not quite through. "The poor sick man told us the very same story we heard from Dzintra a moment ago, the freight train going off, and Hugo running from the farmhouse with milk for his motherless boy, then the endless walking from camp to camp, the endless asking —the despair!"

"Oh, why didn't he come on to Esslingen?" wailed Astra. "It is not far from Würzburg."

"Because he became so ill," Karina explained. She reached over and touched Dzintra, gently. "Listen, dear, Hugo Avots told me he cherished a hope that his son was in good hands. He said, 'That girl who held him when I last saw him—she was a tender little oldmother to my Janis.'"

Dzintra burst into such a soft storm of weeping that her father took the sleeping boy from her, while Mamina gathered her close, whispering, "My linden blossom, there comes an end to the story."

"An end, *jā!*" finished Aina. "For Hugo Avots died, but with a smile on his lips as Karina played for him."

"His violin is among our things in the dormitory," Karina added. "Now it belongs to Janis."

"And Janis now truly belongs to us." Edvarts wiped his eyes. "The boy will be our sacred responsibility. Perhaps he, too, may some day become a fine musician."

"In America I will get work and earn money to pay for Janis' violin lessons," vowed Dzintra, her eyes large and dewy.

Everyone was immediately ready to cry again, but also to laugh tenderly at the thought of eleven-year-old Dzintra wresting from the American economy a paying job, and perhaps working her fingers to the bone for the sake of her beloved brother Janis.

19

SAFE HARBOR

On the last day of 1949, an emigrant ship cleared the port of Bremerhaven and plowed into the wintry waters of the North Sea. Its mission was one of mercy. For at the expense of the United States government, it carried a throng of displaced persons, originally natives of several European countries. Among the two hundred Latvians aboard were Edvarts and Kristine Darzins and their children. Their friends Aina and Karina Ekis were also passengers, bound for the state of Michigan.

"Is Michigan close to Indiana?" asked Dzintra.

Her father shook his head, doubtfully. "Distances are very great in America."

196

But Karina and Astra ran to consult the big map hanging on one of the ship's walls, and returned joyfully to report that the states adjoined. "There is chance, then," concluded Karina, smiling at Astra, "that we shall meet again in the United States."

Almost from the beginning, as the ship entered the rough English Channel, and then the wide Atlantic, most of the passengers suffered seasickness. Dzintra maintained she was spared because she was happy. "Even though I am not on my way to Latvia, and so shall never find the *sakta* my grandmother pledged to me, I am happy because Janis is now my brother forever. I can't be seasick, because I must look after him on this voyage."

Janis became a pet of the ship. The captain called him "a bloomin' cherub," and Dzintra his "guardian angel." The second escort officer, a woman, tweaked the little boy's curls as she hurried about the ship. He was fascinated by the vessel and the vast waters. "When I am grown up," he declared, "I shall be like Captain Olsen and have a big ship. Dzintra, I will take you for a ride."

But this ship was a decrepit old troop transport which had made many crossings. One night the passengers awoke to a strange silence. The beating pulse of the engines had stopped, and therefore the journey. The passengers were frightened almost to panic. Had they striven and sacrificed only to perish in mid-ocean? But the escort officers and nurses moved through the corridors and cabins with cheerful assurances. The necessary repairs were made.

This crisis over, Astra found herself pledged to assist in the preparation of a ship's paper, to be named *The*

Seafarer. In spite of seasickness, copy must be written, edited, multigraphed, and the finished sheets ready for distribution among the passengers before reaching port. The staff of contributors, including an editor-in-chief and a cartoonist, numbered eight, all chosen from among the various nationalities aboard. The two escort officers were to act as advisers.

In the preparation of the Latvian column, Astra worked with a woman named Lilija who had formerly been employed in the administration office at the University of Riga. Lilija expected her young assistant to have ideas.

Astra turned instinctively to her parents. But they were too miserable with seasickness to offer suggestions, although proud that their daughter had been chosen as a co-worker with Lilija. Burdened with a sense of responsibility, Astra could not go to sleep that night. As she lay listening to the creak of the ship and the wintry conflict of wind and water, an old memory came to her. It stole into her mind as on the breath of flowers—a happy, flowery, midsummer morning of long ago, and Marga gay and teasing, singing a snatch from a Latvian folk tune. "That song!" whispered Astra to herself. "If Lilija agrees, it could serve as the keynote to our Latvian article."

So Astra, although often ill herself, was busy with her work on *The Seafarer.* In addition, she must keep an eye on Dzintra and Janis. She must do her expected share and Mamina's, in the cleaning of their cabin and the public rooms. Every day she spent some time with Karina, whom she dearly loved. She posed for the cartoonist, a Hungarian possessed of a delicious sense of humor and a nose most alarming in shape and size.

After ten days at sea, word ran through the transport that the voyage was almost over. Clearing skies and smoother seas contributed to a general uplift of spirits, and the people crept feebly but hopefully to the decks. Copies of *The Seafarer* were passed around and eagerly scanned. The first pages were printed in German for the understanding of all the nationalities aboard. Each of the succeeding articles appeared in the native language of its contributor, with the English translation in the opposite column.

The Czechoslovakian article was a closely spaced history of the country. It expressed the fervent hope that the nation might again become as it had been—glorious. The Estonian editors had been brief. They stated that soon the journey to a free country would be completed, but—"we shall not forget the importance of meeting the fight for the liberty of Estonia, and we ask the Almighty to help."

The Hungarians aboard found voice in blank verse addressed to their patron saint, St. Stephen.

Carefully Lilija and Astra had composed the Latvian column.

In Latvia we have a rich treasure of collected folk songs. As we go to foreign soil to save our lives and to bear witness to tyranny's destruction of nations and people in Europe, one of our folk songs has a special symbolism for us. Part of it goes: "Sing, sing, stranger's daughter. You go sing-

*ing among strangers." But the daughter answers,
"They say life's hard among strangers. I go weeping among strangers."*

*Latvians did not leave their beautiful land to
seek adventure and good luck. We go as serious
men and women, knowing that hard struggle lies
ahead of us in our resolve to rebuild our lives. Having evaded the slave labor camps in Siberia we now
turn our faces toward freedom. We trust our future to America. We will serve it, and in that
service we shall also be serving Latvia, which is
alive in our hearts. So do we go among strangers,
singing in gratitude and hope, weeping in memory
and homesickness. Be good to us, strange country.*

The Seafarer paid compliments to the captain and
crew. There were two pages of humorous cartoons.
The contributors signed their names.

"Here is my daughter's," boasted Edvarts, "also her
picture. But you see how funny the cartoonist has made
her, when really, if you will excuse me, she is like a
flower."

The next morning the cry echoed through the ship.
"Come! Hurry! The Statue of Liberty is in sight! I have
heard it is the world's largest statue. Do you feel as I
do, that it truly welcomes us?"

The Darzins stood grouped together, arms entwined,
faces pale, eyes shining. "The American Liberty is much
larger, but she is not too unlike the great woman who
stands on our own Monument of Liberty in Riga," Edvarts observed.

"Oh, Tevs, Mamina, Dzintra!" cried Astra, softly, "How wonderful is liberty!"

"It is the thing we have sought during six long years of homelessness and suffering," answered Mamina. "At last, in this January of nineteen hundred and fifty, we find in America—*liberty!* Now we are safe."

" 'Be good to us, strange country,' " quoted Dzintra, holding tightly to Janis' hand. While she trembled at the sight of New York's giant towers, and at the thought of the uncertain future ahead, the words held little pathos for her. She said them almost gaily, for like Astra, she was filled with a young and eager hope.

20 IN AMERICA

Spring in America, merging into summer. In America, freedom for refugees to come together in lyrical remembrance of their far, enslaved homeland. "Sing, stranger's daughter." But sing in the sunlight of America's welcome. Sing in freedom.

"We have been in America for over three years, now," wrote Astra to her friend Karina. "On the emigrant ship, and at parting, you and I talked hopefully of an early reunion. So I was disappointed that we could not meet at the song festival in Chicago, the first, as you know, since that final sorrowful one in nineteen hundred and forty, in your own home city in Latvia. Five thousand of our people from all the states and from Canada gathered in Chicago. I attended as a member of the Indianapolis choral group. The festival was most exciting, full of the pageantry of folk-dancing, parades, exhibits, and a vast assemblage of choirs. You should have heard our hymns and beautiful old songs soaring in glory to the American skies. I wore a new costume I had made myself. It seemed strange and touching, Karina, to wear my grandmother Baltais' shawl in a parade on a Chicago boulevard."

June in America. A midsummer country celebration in a setting of American wheat fields, acres wide, golden with ripening. Haunting memories of Latvian pine forests in which the midnight fern blooms for lovers on St. John's Eve. The traditional St. John's fire; the dancing and the singing; the old folk rhymes. "Wear your wreath proudly, young girl, but more proudly wear this golden ring of mine."

It was after the St. John's Eve celebration that Astra made an announcement.

"Astra Darzins! Keeping the news of your engagement from us for a whole week!" Dzintra pouted. "Well, anyway," she added, triumphantly, "I'm sure I saw you and Rolands Kruze falling in love that day on the old castle stairs in Esslingen!"

"We are glad, *milumin.*" Mamina put her arms around the radiant Astra. "Rolands is already like a son to us."

"*Jā,* but my little girl is not old enough to get married!" cried Tevs.

"She will soon be twenty-three," Mamina reminded him.

Tevs seemed so astonished that everyone laughed. But he recovered briskly. "The time has come," he said, "to make a bride's *sakta*." Fluttering his fingers airily, he described how delicate it would be with pearls and crystals.

Astra ran to kiss his cheek. "Dear, you need not hurry with my bridal *sakta,* any more than with Dzintra's amber-set ring we have promised her three years from now, when she graduates from high school. Rolands and I also need three years to get our college degrees. We have vowed no wedding bells until then."

"But in the meantime Rolands' green thumb works well for him?" inquired Tevs.

"*Jā,*" answered Astra, smiling. "And for his employer, who is very pleased. Rolands finds surprising satisfaction in tending the gardens and greenhouses. But we hope some day to buy the photography business he dreams about."

That night Dzintra lay in bed, thinking, with a premature loneliness, about Astra leaving home. She raised herself on one elbow to gaze at her sleeping sister, whose face was illuminated by moonlight shining through the windows. The night's poetry entered into Dzintra. "My sister has more than prettiness. Sometimes, especially when she is with the Latvians here, and quiet among them, I see on her face a most beautiful look. I can't describe it. It is a look clear but shadowed, deep yet exalted. What does it mean? . . . Latvia, and Astra's memories of Latvia? . . . Marga? . . . Astra's love and

sorrow for Marga which has somehow turned into a
beautiful strength? . . . *Jā,* I am glad I thought of that.
. . . Dear Astra! I hope that Rolands appreciates his
great good luck!"

*Deep summer. American corn in tall, green ranks.
American apples ripening. Remembering a Latvian orchard; remembering a beloved granny's words—"Dzintra's apples shall drop into her hands like gifts." Granny!
Vecmamina!*

It was Janis who opened the door one evening in answer to Pastor Schoen's knock.

"*Labvaker,* my friends!" cried the American, jubilant
as a child because he could say "good-evening" in Latvian. "How comfortable you are here! I see you have
new wall paper."

"We papered the walls ourselves, Pastor," stated Edvarts. "We take pride in a house of our own, although
paying for it will be a long stretch."

"Courage!" advised the pastor. "You are all employed.
Even Dzintra, I hear, has a part-time summer job."

"*Jā,* we are proud of her," said Mamina. "We are all
fortunate to be doing work which we like. So many DP's,
especially those who had professions in their homeland,
are unhappy here because they must engage in uncon-
genial employment. But my husband works in jewelry
and engraving as he did in Riga, although not yet in a
shop of his own. Our Astra is more than useful in church
office work."

"Under your praise, Kristine, we are about to swell up
and burst!" joked Tevs.

"Pastor Schoen," wailed Janis, "we have been in America for three years, and I do not yet have work! Won't you please tell my parents how I could help pay for our house if only they would let me have a newspaper route?"

"You are only eight years old, my son. Hold your patience for the paper route you shall have some day," promised Tevs.

"Then go ahead, Mamina," said Janis, mollified. "Tell about your job."

When Mamina only laughed, Astra turned to the pastor. "It takes courage for our mother to sell shoes. She thinks we do not guess how much she loathes it."

"Ah, but she was born brave!" cried Tevs. "You cannot know, Pastor Schoen, how she endured, and was brave and gay for our sakes through all our troubles."

"Hush, now!" Mamina's cheeks were pink. "I sell shoes, politely and with my might. We came penniless to America. We need money to exchange for clothing, and for the food in the super markets. We are buying this house. Some day we shall buy nice rugs and furniture to replace the things given to us when we came to Indianapolis."

"That reminds me, Pastor Schoen," said Dzintra, "of our first evening in the three-room apartment you had got for us. It was February, and we were stiff with cold and strangeness. The apartment was beautifully warm. A beef and vegetable stew was simmering in the kitchen. Two smiling American ladies waited to welcome us. After they left, Astra and Janis and I went around in a daze, touching things and peeping into drawers, whispering, 'Tevs and Mamina, these things are really ours?' "

"After all our wanderings, and our worry as to what America would be like, we found kindness," Mamina said.

"To remember and rejoice in kindness is good," said the pastor. "But Edvarts, I have waited too long to tell you. I have a letter here. It was sent by the Red Cross to Lutheran headquarters and then to me. It bears a March date and a Swedish postmark."

"Swedish?" Puzzled, Tevs took the letter, turning it about in his hands until Janis demanded that he open it. Then how Tevs stared at the handwriting! He jumped to his feet, waving the sheet, almost babbling. "This letter is from my brother Imants! Do you hear, Kristine? After nine years, my own mother—"

"You mean our dear vecmamina?" cried Dzintra. "Tevs, read the letter!"

"I have read it!" shouted Tevs. "I swallowed it in one gulp, like a starving man! Your uncle Imants and your granny Darzins escaped to Sweden right after Riga fell to the Communists. In an open boat, with twelve other fugitives—jā, Imants writes of the hardship suffered in that thirty-hour voyage across the wintry Baltic Sea. But at last they sighted the island of Gotland."

Tevs began reading from the letter: " 'How we laughed and shouted! We were free! We could sing the Latvian hymn again! We did, and were not afraid. Some Swedish fishermen saw and heard us. They towed us ashore. The next day we came to the mainland of Sweden. Here we live in peace, thanking God every hour.' "

When the family's tears and laughter had subsided a little, Tevs went on. "As soon as he hears that we still live, and where, Imants promises to send us something he calls 'precious.' I can't imagine what it may be, unless our cow, Brune." Tevs bubbled with gaiety.

"You must send an answer to your kin by air-mail at once," advised Pastor Schoen. His face beamed with pleasure.

"Joy on the wing—that will be our letter," sighed Mamina.

September in America. School. Astra struggling with an English theme, with names she had never heard—Byron, Keats, Shelley—yet drawing into herself the glory of their poetry. . . . Dzintra studious and quick, striving for a scholarship; gay at American parties; falling easily into American ways, falling in love with America. . . . Janis, enchanted with his American cowboy suit, his holster and pistol, with American lollipops; excited by American superlatives—the grandest canyon, the oldest trees, the largest telescope, the most money; Janis saluting with little-boy gravity the stars-and-stripes, revering Washington and Lincoln.

"Tevs, I'm an American," boasted Janis.

"You have Latvian blood," Tevs protested.

"But it doesn't show," declared Janis. "I'm not going to talk Latvian any more. As long as I do, I'm not a *pure* American. Tevs, it will be too bad when you and I don't even speak the same language. You see, you must talk American, too."

Tevs flinched noticeably. For a moment Mamina came

to his defense. "Who could be so unfaithful as to forget our dear Latvian words?" she asked. "But Janis is right, Edvarts. You should learn English. What kind of an American citizen will you make, if you can say only, 'hello-okay?' "

"I always carry my little Latvian-English dictionary in my pocket," Tevs blustered. "I get along."

"Not well," scolded Astra. "I have seen you at a complete loss, even with your dictionary."

"Let your daughters and your son teach you, Tevs," Dzintra offered.

"Never can I twist my mouth into such contortions! Never—oh, well—jā, it will be a battle, but for my son I will try."

October in America, each blue-and-gold day a gift of beauty. American hardwoods flaunting colors in red and russet, yellow and amber.

Tevs' hands shook a little as he unwrapped the box from Sweden that October day. Almost gingerly he lifted the lid. On a bed of cotton gleamed something which he took out and laid reverently in Mamina's hand. She gazed at it, her eyes wide and unbelieving. Then she was weeping—Mamina weeping! After a gasp of recognition, neither could Astra keep back her tears.

Dzintra began to tremble. That beautiful thing in Mamina's hand—nē, it couldn't be! But Mamina was wiping her eyes. She was saying to Dzintra, "Take it, my daughter. This is your grandmother's *sakta* which you thought never to have."

Dzintra held the brooch, gazing at it speechlessly, and

for a moment she had the strange sensation that her grandmother Baltais was there beside her. "Mamina," she whispered, "it is a miracle! Oh, Mamina, this *sakta* shall be my dearest, dearest treasure!"

For several days the Darzins could talk of little else. What was the true story of the *sakta*?

A letter of explanation arrived from Vecmamina. "Eriks Baltais brought the *sakta* to our apartment in Riga," she wrote. "It was soon after you left. He said that one night, as he lay half-asleep in a forest, he suddenly remembered the *sakta's* hiding place, of which his grandmother had told him. Recalling her pledge to Dzintra, he resolved to go after the jewel, although he knew what a hazardous thing it would be for an underground Freedom Fighter to travel through the Communist-infested land. But Eriks did it by some miracle of stealth and caution. He told me nothing about his experiences in getting the *sakta* from the Baltais farm. From there he went to your house in Vidzeme, and found it in ashes. Doggedly, then, he made his way to Riga, and was overjoyed to learn from us that you had escaped.

"Eriks was greatly changed, very thin, wearing a beard, looking much older. He never smiled once in the brief time he was with us. He sent you a message, in case we ever found you. He said, 'Tell them, though I die, my love for them is undying.' Then he was gone, as swiftly and secretly as he had come. Brave Eriks—long ago he must have perished for Latvia."

The American month of Thanksgiving. The early Pilgrims; the late pilgrims. Through the years, countless pilgrims seeking new life in a new land. . . . *Now, in November . . . Now, in America . . .*

"My son, it is plain that you are to be a wholehearted American. But your roots are in Latvia," Tevs explained. "Tonight, as always, we celebrate the founding of the Latvian Free Republic, which took place in November, nineteen hundred and eighteen."

"Free?" questioned Janis.

"No longer free," answered Tevs. "But Latvia's liberation is our living hope. So we keep on celebrating, even here in America, whose citizens we shall be. And something more. Tonight we pay honor to our kin and countrymen who were killed, or deported to slave labor camps. Do you understand, son?"

"I think so, Tevs. Yet Astra and Dzintra will dance tonight?"

"They will dance. In the midst of our harsh memories we have reason to rejoice. We shall present our best dancing and singing to the American guests."

Astra had overheard this conversation. It was still in her mind as she stood on the stage of the rented hall with her fellow-choristers an hour later. It seemed to have created in her an extraordinary sensitivity to the significance of tonight's anniversary, the new life in America, and the old one in Latvia. She imagined that from her vantage point on the stage she was able to look into hearts as well as faces. When the choir sang "The Star-Spangled Banner," Astra understood and pitied the resigned loneliness of the many Latvians in the audience to whom the English words meant nothing. The quick tears on the cheeks of some of the American guests revealed to her how touched they were at hearing their beloved anthem sung by refugees from a far country. She saw their polite interest in the Latvian hymn, and the shining response of the Latvians themselves. The flags of the two nations, side-by-side on their standards, seemed to Astra beautifully symbolic of friendship and equality.

There were speeches both in Latvian and English, memorial addresses full of dignity and reverence, and one of fiery resentment against Communist tyranny.

It was a relief to hear Pastor Schoen's quiet voice. Listening, Astra's thoughts turned hopefully to the life she expected to have with Rolands, and with their children who would be American-born.

"My friends," said the pastor, "lend freely to us the rich culture of Latvia. Borrow from us our best. Cherish your deep and natural love for the old land, but give the new one your faith and loyalty. Fulfill honestly the obligations of your American citizenship. May peace and security come to all the world."

Astra's heart was light as she joined the choir in the final singing. With the familiar Baltic words on her lips a thought came to her, fanciful yet warmly exultant. "If I might, I would sing a little solo to these people. Not the old, sad folk lyric, 'I sing among strangers.' Nē, not that, but a glad new one of my own— 'I sing among friends.'"

This fancy lingered pleasantly in her mind as she joined the other folk dancers. She and Rolands paired together as they had at Esslingen, but with a deeper joy. Often, in the changing patterns of the dances, she touched hands with Dzintra, radiant in her festive costume, the precious *sakta* glowing on her embroidered vest.

When the celebration was over, many from the audience came to offer their compliments. Astra noticed how Pastor Schoen had a special greeting for each performer. He came to Astra. "I have watched you singing and dancing tonight for our pleasure. My dear, I think you may have found happiness in this country," observed the pastor.

Astra's glance flew to Rolands, to Tevs and Mamina, to Dzintra and Janis. It swept over the friendly, smiling people. "*Jā*, Pastor, in America I am happy."

Even as she said it, and knew that it was gloriously true, an old pain smote her heart.

BIBLIOGRAPHY

The Daina, U. Katzenelenbogen. Lithuanian News Publishing Company, Inc., Chicago, 1935.

Book of Festivals, Dorothy Gladys Spicer. The Woman's Press, 1937.

Dictionary of Events in Latvia, Alfreds Bilmanis (formerly Latvian Minister Plenipotentiary to the United States). Latvian Legation Press, Washington, D.C., 1946.

Latvia as an Independent State, Alfreds Bilmanis. Latvian Legation Press, Washington, D.C., 1947.

History of Latvia, Alfreds Bilmanis. Princeton University Press, 1951.

Latvia, Country and People, R.O.G. Urch. Riga, Walter, 1935.

Displaced Persons. Hearings before the Subcommittee on Amendments to the Displaced Persons Act. United States Senate. Eighty-first Congress.